WITHDRAWN

NELSON MANDELA AND THE END OF APARTHEID

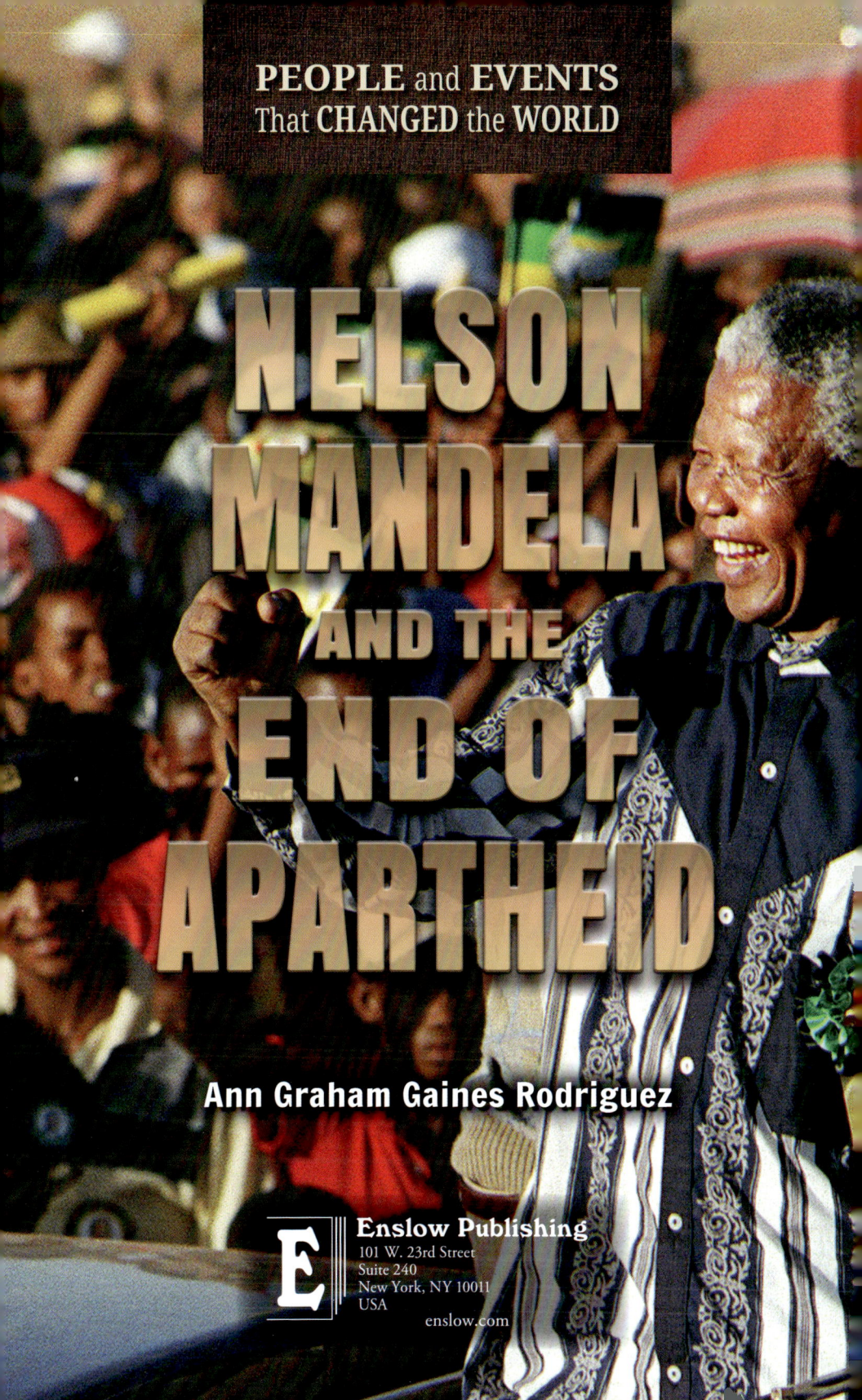

PEOPLE and EVENTS That CHANGED the WORLD

NELSON MANDELA AND THE END OF APARTHEID

Ann Graham Gaines Rodriguez

Enslow Publishing
101 W. 23rd Street
Suite 240
New York, NY 10011
USA

enslow.com

Published in 2016 by Enslow Publishing, LLC
101 W. 23rd Street, Suite 240, New York, NY 10011

Copyright © 2016 by Ann Graham Gaines Rodriguez

All rights reserved.

No part of this book may be reproduced by any means without the written permission of the publisher.

Library of Congress Cataloging-in-Publication Data
Gaines Rodriguez, Ann Graham, author.
 Nelson Mandela and the end of apartheid / Ann Graham Gaines Rodriguez.
    pages cm. — (People and events that changed the world)
 Includes bibliographical references and index.
 Audience: Grade 9 to 12.
 ISBN 978-0-7660-7300-5
 1. Mandela, Nelson, 1918-2013—Juvenile literature. 2. Presidents—South Africa—Biography—Juvenile literature. 3. Anti-apartheid activists—South Africa—Biography—Juvenile literature. 4. Apartheid—South Africa—History—20th century—Juvenile literature. 5. South Africa—Politics and government—1948-1994—Juvenile literature. 6. South Africa—Politics and government—1994—Juvenile literature. 7. South Africa—Race relations—History—20th century—Juvenile literature. I. Title.
 DT1974.G36 2016
 305.800968'09045—dc23
                    2015030868

Printed in the United States of America

To Our Readers: We have done our best to make sure all website addresses in this book were active and appropriate when we went to press. However, the author and the publisher have no control over and assume no liability for the material available on those websites or on any websites they may link to. Any comments or suggestions can be sent by e-mail to customerservice@enslow.com.

Portions of this book originally appeared in the book *Nelson Mandela and Apartheid in World History*.

Photo Credits: Cover, p. 3 GUY TILLIM/AFP/Getty Images; EdwardSV/Shutterstock.com (series logo background and headers throughout book), Graphico imaginarea/Shutterstock.com (South African flag on spine); p. 6 David Levenson/Hulton Archive/Getty Images; p. 12 Rainer Lesniewski/Shutterstock.com; p. 16 The Print Collector/Print Collector/Hulton Archive/Getty Images; p. 20 Hulton Archive/Getty Images; p. 25 Rischgitz/Hulton Archive/Getty Images; p. 31 john michael evan potter/Shutterstock.com; pp. 35, 65 FPG/Archive Photos/Getty Images; p. 39 CARL DE SOUZA/AFP/Getty Images; p. 42 Fountain Posters/Wikimedia Commons/Young Mandela.jpg/public domain; pp. 46, 74 Keystone-France/Gamma-Keystone/Getty Images; p. 49 Bob Landry/The LIFE Picture Collection/Getty Images; p. 53 Popperfoto/Popperfoto/Getty Images; p. 56 Gallo Images/Hulton Archives/Getty Images; p. 61 Three Lions/Hulton Archive/Getty Images; p. 69 Topical Press Agency/Hulton Archive/Getty Images; p. 72 Apic/Hulton Archive/Getty Images; p. 76 OFF/AFP/Getty Images; p. 78 Central Press/Hulton Archive/ Getty Images; p. 82 STF/AFP/Getty Images; p. 86 Shaun Botterill/Getty Images Sport/Getty Images; p. 91 Central Press/Hulton Archive/Getty Images; pp. 94, 101 TREVOR SAMSON/AFP/Getty Images; p. 96 City Press/Gallo Images/Getty Images; p. 99 RASHID LOMBARD/AFP/Getty Images; p. 104 Media24/Gallo Images/Getty Images; p. 106 THEMBA HADEBE/AFP/Getty Images; p. 111 Kyodo via AP Images.

CONTENTS

CHAPTER 1	An End to a Fight—and a Peace Prize	7
CHAPTER 2	South Africa's Past	11
CHAPTER 3	A Young Nelson Mandela	30
CHAPTER 4	The Rise of Apartheid	45
CHAPTER 5	Apartheid—"Apartness"	58
CHAPTER 6	Fighting Back	67
CHAPTER 7	Arrested and Imprisoned	81
CHAPTER 8	Freedom for Mandela and His People	93
CHAPTER 9	In Retirement	105
	Timeline	113
	Chapter Notes	116
	Glossary	123
	Further Reading	125
	Index	126

Nelson Mandela and Frederik de Klerk were the joint recipients of the Nobel Peace Prize in 1993.

CHAPTER 1

An End to a Fight— and a Peace Prize

On October 15, 1993, the Nobel Foundation announced the recipients of that year's Peace Prize. To the world's surprise, the prize would go to political opponents, South Africans Nelson Mandela, long-time political prisoner, and Frederik W. de Klerk, the country's leader. They received this great honor because, despite their differences, they had fought together to end oppression in South Africa. Together they had overturned apartheid, a terrible system of segregation that the South African government had used for forty years.

Two months later, in December of 1993, the men celebrated at a ceremony in Oslo, Sweden. After it was finished, the two stood side by side showing off their medals. They differed greatly in appearance and background. Mandela was a stately, gray-haired, seventy-five-year-old black man. De Klerk was a fifty-seven-year-old, balding, white man. Both had been born to influential families. De Klerk's great-grandfather, grandfather, and father had all been important in South African politics. Mandela's father had been a tribal chief. However, the two men had hardly grown up in the same way.

NELSON MANDELA and the END of APARTHEID

De Klerk was an Afrikaner—a white South African with Dutch ancestors, who spoke the Afrikaans language. From boyhood on, he had enjoyed a life of privilege, never wanting for food or shelter. He had plenty of money to buy luxuries. He had had a tremendously successful political career, and was elected president of South Africa in 1989.

Mandela, on the other hand, had endured a hard life. He had suffered hunger and other discomforts. As a young man, he had seen many of his opportunities vanish when the South African government put into place new restrictions on black South Africans. Mandela became just one of millions of victims of apartheid, which forced blacks and other nonwhites to live in separate communities and obey separate laws. Over time, Mandela became a leader among those who fought against apartheid. He was arrested and tried for his actions and imprisoned for twenty-seven years. But even behind bars, he continued to fight for the rights of his people. While in prison, he became a symbolic figure, an inspiration both to black South Africans fighting for their rights and to other human rights activists around the globe. When he finally left prison in 1990, the news made headlines around the world.

In its announcement concerning the prize, the Nobel Peace Prize committee said that both Mandela and de Klerk had "personal integrity and great political courage."[1] It awarded them the peace prize because, after a difficult struggle, they had finally brought about radical political change in South Africa.

The South African government, which had held Mandela in prison since 1962, had expressed interest in releasing Mandela from prison in 1985. Other countries put pressure on South Africa to do so. But Mandela had refused to leave

An End to a Fight—and a Peace Prize

prison unless certain conditions were met. Although he wanted freedom, he knew his imprisonment was a powerful political symbol. He wanted apartheid ended and the political organizations that had been banned to be allowed to meet once again. The president before de Klerk, Pieter Botha, had never been willing to meet Mandela's demands. But de Klerk was.

The year after his election as president, de Klerk had ordered Mandela released from prison. Then Mandela and de Klerk began to work together to end apartheid. The Nobel committee said it had awarded the prize in recognition of achievements Mandela and de Klerk had made thus far. It wanted the award to be seen "as a pledge of support for the forces of good, in the hope that the advance towards equality and democracy will reach its goal in the very near future."[2]

When the prize was announced, Mandela and de Klerk were actually engaged in political battle. Together they had succeeded in bringing about the first election in decades in which black South Africans would be able to vote along with whites. But the two men belonged to different political parties. Each was seeking to become president of South Africa.

Each man expressed great joy when the announcement was made that jointly they would receive the Nobel Prize. De Klerk was relieved that he had brought his government through a difficult period. Mandela took an even longer view. Interested in the history of his people from the time he was a child, he saw himself as part of a fight that had been going on for five hundred years. He considered himself the representative of millions of people who had dared to fight for their rights. He knew it was the protests of many black and other nonwhite South Africans that was bringing apartheid to an end.

In the speech Mandela delivered when he received the Nobel Prize, he spoke of his hope that the black children of South Africa would soon no longer suffer from hunger or disease, and that they could finally receive a decent education. Their parents would no longer fear being arrested, imprisoned, tortured, or killed for fighting for their rights.

Mandela later summed up his own life, writing:

> I have walked [a] long road to freedom. I have tried not to falter; I have made missteps along the way. But I have discovered the secret that after climbing a great hill, one only finds that there are many more hills to climb. I have taken a moment here to rest, to steal a view of the glorious vista that surrounds me, to look back on the distance I have come.[3]

Mandela enjoyed his freedom. But he knew there was much more for him to do. He wanted to help South Africa create a new society. And so he said, "But I can rest only for a moment, for with freedom comes responsibilities, and I dare not linger, for my long walk is not yet ended."[4]

CHAPTER 2

South Africa's Past

Nelson Mandela changed South Africa forever. It is only through learning about South Africa, the land and its history, that one can fully understand why it was so important—and difficult—to win freedom for its long-oppressed people.

The Place and Its People

The modern nation of South Africa sits on the southernmost section of the continent of Africa. Bordered on the Atlantic Ocean to the west, and the Indian Ocean to the east, it features a narrow coastal plain. Inland lies high plateaus, bordered by a mountain range known as the High Escarpment.

South Africa is large, both in terms of its size and its population. There are close to two hundred nations in the world. South Africa ranks twenty-fifth in terms of territory and twenty-eighth in terms of population.[1] In 2014 South Africa had a population of approximately forty-nine million. Of those, forty million were classified as black, 4.5 million as mixed race (designated "coloured" in the South African census) and five million were white. Despite the much

NELSON MANDELA and the END of APARTHEID

Modern South Africa is located at the southernmost tip of Africa and bordered by the Atlantic and Indian Oceans.

South Africa's Past

larger number of people of color, for many years, the white minority held all political power.

As a nation, South Africa is also distinguished by its wealth. It exports more gold than any other nation. But even now that apartheid has ended, 20% of the population live in extreme poverty.[2]

Long Ago

Archeologists have found evidence of modern humans living in what is now South Africa one hundred thousand years ago. For tens of thousands of years, the native peoples of South Africa were hunter-gatherers. About two thousand years ago, people known as the Khoikhoi, or Hottentots, began to raise livestock. Societies evolved that valued livestock very highly. Leaders were those who owned the most sheep and cattle.

A thousand years ago, people in southern Africa belonged to many different clans. They spoke a variety of languages. Even today, black South Africans consider themselves members of clans, rather than a single race.

From its beginning, the history of South Africa has been characterized by conflict. Some of these conflicts have gone on for generations. Most have been over land. Some especially valuable resources, such as water, have also caused many fights among the people of South Africa.

Europeans Visit South Africa for the First Time

What would become the nation of South Africa was visited first by the Portuguese. Toward the end of the fifteenth century, Portugal was searching for an eastward sea route to the East Indies. They wanted to go there to buy spices not found in Europe, that could be sold back home for high prices. In 1488 Bartholomew Diaz commanded ships that sailed south around the Cape of Good Hope, the southern tip of the continent of Africa. On February 3, 1488, his expedition made landfall. This was when natives of southern Africa saw Europeans for the first time.

In 1495 explorer Vasco da Gama finally succeeded in sailing around Africa to reach the Indies. His first encounter with natives in South Africa was friendly. They traded with each other. Although a misunderstanding arose in which the Khoikhoi wounded three or four of da Gama's Portuguese with spears, da Gama and his company would land in southern Africa three more times.

The Portuguese dominated the spice trade for about a century. Their ships continued to land in southern Africa, but the Portuguese showed no interest in building a colony there. The area could not give them the spices and ivory they were looking for. They did not realize then that there was a great deal of gold in Africa.

In 1595 a Dutchman named Cornelius Houtman sailed around the Cape of Good Hope. By this time, sailors from many European nations were making the voyage around the southern tip of Africa. But it was the Dutch who eventually took control of the spice trade from the Portuguese.

In the early seventeenth century, both Dutch and British trading companies sent ships to the East Indies. One big problem faced the captains of their ships. The voyage took so long that their crews ran out of fresh water, fruits and vegetables (sailors needed fruits and vegetables or they suffered from the disease called scurvy), and other supplies. They needed a place to stock up on supplies during the voyage. South Africa was a logical place for them to make a regular stop.

In 1619 representatives of the Dutch East India Company and the British East India Company met to discuss their mutual need for a stop on the way to the Indies, where ships could rest their sailors and buy new supplies. Although talks took place, it would take decades for the idea to take root.

A Colony Is Established

The first successful attempt to establish a calling station in southern Africa resulted from an accident. In 1647, a Dutch ship named the *Haarlem* was wrecked in Table Bay on the southwest coast of Africa. Its crew went ashore and settled nearby. It took six months for them to be rescued. In the meantime, the sailors got along very well. There was fresh water there. They grew vegetables and traded for meat with the Khoikhoi who lived in the area. When the men of the *Haarlem* crew returned to the Netherlands in 1649, they spoke very positively about their time in South Africa. Their company decided they had found a good spot to build a place for ships to stop on the route to the Indies.[3]

On June 4, 1652, an expedition led by Jan van Riebeeck reached Table Bay. He had brought with him three ships and 130 men and women. These settlers had been instructed to build a fort where they could keep a supply of fresh water and grow fruits and vegetables. They were also supposed to establish trade with the Khoikhoi for cattle and sheep, and they had orders to build a hospital.

The purpose of the settlement was to serve ships that stopped at Table Bay. The colony was sponsored by the Dutch East India Company, not the Dutch government. The government had given the corporation a charter giving it

NELSON MANDELA and the END of APARTHEID

The Khoikhoi had a peaceful relationship with white settlers when they first arrived in southern Africa. Here, the natives trade cattle with the settlers.

rights over the land in and east of the Cape of Good Hope. The company's establishment of a colony there was a business move, designed to make East Indies trade easier—and more profitable.[4]

The settlers suffered terribly at first. A drought made gardening difficult and led to starvation. At first, the Khoikhoi did not want to trade with the Dutch for animals. Within weeks, fifteen white settlers had died. Half of those who survived became so sick from dysentery, a terrible disease of the lower intestine, that they could not work. Soon, however, the situation improved. The settlers were able to trade for both meat and vegetables. Within fifty years, these white colonists, who would become known as Boers or Afrikaners, had begun to develop their own language, called Afrikaans. In 1657 the Dutch East India Company imported eleven slaves to do hard labor for settlers, such as clearing fields and building.[5] Slavery then increased at a rapid rate.

Slaves were brought in on ships. Some were from other parts of Africa, but many were from Madagascar, Indonesia, India, and Ceylon. The company used slaves to build roads and do other labor, like building up riverbanks. Officials and well-to-do people came to depend on slaves to work in their houses, get wood and water, and plant gardens. Slaves worked in the fields on farms and plantations. By 1708 there were more than one thousand slaves in the colony. In 1793 the population of South Africa was 30,000. Of that number, 14,747 were slaves.

At the beginning of the colonial era, there were some free blacks in the colony. Some slaves had been freed. But this would happen less often as time went by. Slavery would continue in the colony for more than one hundred fifty years.

By 1800 the colony that had begun at Table Bay had greatly expanded. The European population numbered around fifteen thousand.[6] The colony's population included not only Afrikaners and slaves, but many other people whom the whites called Coloured. These people included those who had both black and white ancestors.

When the Dutch settlers first arrived in 1652, the African natives were not particularly affected by them. The colonists treated the natives in a friendly manner so that they would trade cattle. The Dutch also believed there was enough land to share. After the Dutch were able to raise their own livestock, however, they no longer needed to treat the native Khoikhoi people carefully. White colonists began to try to push the natives off their land in order to expand the Dutch colony.

First, white farmers would move beyond the colony's boundaries, looking for new land that had water and was easy to plow. Once they had set down roots, the colonial government would then make the land they had taken over part of the colony. The settlers did meet resistance, but they won many of the fights they had with the native Bushmen and Khoikhoi who defended what had long been their land. The Dutch had many guns. The natives had just the small number of firearms the Dutch had traded them. The Khoikhoi also suffered terribly during a smallpox epidemic in 1713. Many native people agreed to move in order to avoid further contact with the Europeans. When expansion continued onto their lands, Bantu speakers such as the Xhosa people fought to keep their land. Both sides suffered deaths in fighting between Afrikaners and natives in 1779 and 1793.

The British Take Over

In 1794 the Dutch East India Company declared bankruptcy, after years of struggling with money troubles. The British saw this as their chance to take over the colony in South Africa. The Dutch who had settled there wanted to stay and rule the colony they had started, but in 1795, British troops captured the Cape Colony, as the Dutch settlement was known. The Dutch briefly won back the colony in 1803, but that would last for only a short time. The British Navy sent sixty-one warships to recapture the Cape Colony in 1806. Meanwhile, the Xhosa people had been fighting the white colonists once more, trying to hold onto their land. In 1803, the Xhosa defeated the Afrikaners.

After the British took over the Cape Colony in 1806, British government officials arrived to govern. The governor acknowledged the Khoikhoi as residents of the colony, but also established constraints for them. The natives were not regarded as slaves, but apprentices. In order to move about, they had to get passes from their employers or the farmers whose land they worked.

The first British settlers arrived in 1820. The Xhosa continued to challenge white settlers along the colony's borders. In 1834 the Karrir War took place, between the natives and the British. Both sides had been making raids, stealing cattle from their enemies. This, however, became a full-scale war in which many people died. The Xhosa finally won.

After the war, the colony's governor started a new province. The government reached an agreement with Xhosa chiefs in which the Xhosa were allowed to live in the

The Xhosa people were forced to defend their land from various settlers over the years. This scene shows the Xhosa returning from one of these conflicts.

white-governed province. In exchange, the Xhosa had to become British subjects and give up their weapons.

Throughout this period, European settlers generally looked upon native Africans as an inferior race of people, worthy only to serve and work for white men. However, missionaries pressured the British government of the area to grant Africans rights. They succeeded in 1828. The 50th Ordinance was passed. It granted civil rights to free nonwhites.[7]

Primary Source: A Doctor's View of the Xhosa

Every day King Williams Town was thronged and its inhabitants distressed at the sight of emaciated living skeletons passing from house to house. Dead bodies were picked up in different parts within and around the limits of the towns, and scarcely a day passed over, that men, women or children were not found in a dying state from starvation.

My consulting room was every day surrounded with emaciated creatures craving food, having nothing to subsist on but roots and the bark of the mimosa, the smell of which appeared to issue from every party of the body, and to whim it would be a mockery to say, you must seek employment, or proceed on to the colony.

–Dr. John Fitzgerald describes the Xhosa he saw, who resisted Dutch and British incursion into their land [8]

Afrikaaners' Revolt

By this time, settlers of Dutch descent had become very unhappy with the British government that now ruled the South African colony. Ever since the days of the Dutch East India Company, the Afrikaners had forced slaves to work in their fields and their houses. In 1833, however, the British Parliament in London ruled that all slaves in the British Empire—including those in South Africa—had to be freed.

Afrikaners were extremely angry at this news. They were upset, too, when Parliament made English the colony's official language. Then, an official in Great Britain decided that the colony's governor should not have created the new province, meaning that the land taken from natives would have to be given back. The Dutch regarded this as a final blow.

By 1836 the Afrikaners had begun to move out of the colony and into the land that had been turned back over to native Africans. This migration became known as the Great Trek. Those who took part in it were called *trekboers*. Settlers traveled north and east in several groups, along three routes.

Along the way, they met natives who were willing to fight for their land and their way of life. The Zulu of an area called Natal fought especially ferociously. However, trekkers finally defeated them and received a large part of the Natal district as a result. In other areas, trekkers found unpopulated land on which to settle. In most cases, former inhabitants had died or had been forced to flee during their own native wars with the Zulu.

The trekkers established the Republic of Natal. From the beginning, the native black population was much larger than

South Africa's Past

the white population in Natal. In 1845 the British declared that Great Britain, not Dutch trekkers, owned the Republic. The colonial government then established reserves—blocks of land the government set aside as places only blacks could live. This left good land free for white settlers. Reserves would soon be established elsewhere, too.

Throughout the colonial history of South Africa, the government left tribal chiefs in place to govern their own people. Natives continued to hope that the Europeans would someday leave. In the middle of the nineteenth century, for example, the Xhosa killed their cattle and planted no crops, hoping to upset their ancestors enough to make them rise from the dead and chase the white settlers into the sea.[9]

In reaction to the British takeover of Natal, the Dutch fled and moved with other trekkers to the area between the Orange and the Vaal rivers. There, they established another independent nation, known as the South African Republic, or Transvaal. Trekkers also set up the Orange Free State, in 1854. Soon, in-fighting caused Afrikaners to establish three more tiny republics, bringing the total of their republics to five. By this time, the British had three separate colonies in what would later become South Africa: Cape Colony, Natal, and British Kaffraria. Eventually, all these political units—both Afrikaners and British—would unite to become the modern nation of South Africa.

In the 1860s, the British started to bring Indian laborers to their southern Africa plantations. Indians soon came to make up a significant portion of the South African population.

In the 1860s and 1870s, the affairs of the Afrikaners' South African Republic were in an uproar. A president had been forced to step down. The British decided that the country was weak. In 1877, without the Afrikaners' agreement, the British annexed the South African Republic. This action caused a great feeling of nationalism to rise among the Dutch settlers. In 1880 the Transvaal War of Independence began. Afrikaners defeated British soldiers at the Battle of Majuba Hills on February 27, 1881. However, peace did not come right away. Six months later, the British granted Afrikaners the right to govern Transvaal as long as they accepted British overrule. In other words, Transvaal became a British colony ruled locally by Afrikaners.

In the meantime, a new player—Germany—had arrived on the scene in southern Africa. After Germany formed from many formerly independent states in 1871, it also wanted to expand. German settlers began to emigrate to Africa. Eventually, Germans ruled East Africa (which would later become Tanzania), Cameroon, and the new South West Africa.

One reason so many European powers were interested in controlling this area of the world was that diamonds had been discovered in South Africa in 1870. Interest increased even more after gold was discovered in 1885.

In 1890 Cecil Rhodes became prime minister of the Cape Colony. At first, Rhodes wanted Great Britain to rule all of Africa. Later, he would come to believe that South Africans should be allowed self-rule.

In 1895 Rhodes was shipping arms to British settlers in Transvaal, who were planning a rebellion against the area's Dutch government. At the same time, he ordered a British settler named Dr. Leander Jameson to invade the Transvaal. Jameson was captured, however, and the British residents of Transvaal did not rebel. Transvaal remained Dutch.

South Africa's Past

A depiction of fighting between the British and Afrikaners during the South African War, or Boer War.

Rhodes was forced to resign. The Orange Free State and the Transvaal then decided to fight the British together.

The South African War (or the Boer War)

What the British called the Boer War then broke out. (Afrikaners called it the Second War of Freedom.) Today, historians generally call it the South African War. In October 1899, Paul Kruger, the president of Transvaal, notified the British that he wanted their troops to move away from Transvaal's border. When the British did not obey, fighting broke out.

The Afrikaners were better prepared for war than the British were. They did well at first. However, the British had many more troops available.

The Afrikaners suffered terribly during the fighting, which happened in Transvaal, the Orange Free State, Natal, Zululand, and the Cape Colony. The British government adopted a "scorched earth policy."[10] It ordered the burning of Afrikaner crops and homes and sent the thousands of people left with no place to live to concentration, or prison, camps. More than twenty thousand Afrikaners—mostly women and children—died of disease there.

The war also took a tremendous toll on black South Africans. Estimates of the number of blacks who fought for the British are as high as fifteen thousand. More than one hundred thousand blacks—including women and children—who had been living under the Afrikaner government also ended up in concentration camps.[11]

The war finally ended when British and Afrikaner representatives signed the Peace of Vereeniging on May 21, 1902. The Boer republics became British colonies. However, the British promised that the Afrikaners could soon run their own local governments again. The treaty guaranteed that most of those who had fought for the Afrikaners would not be treated as traitors or punished for having fought against the British. Those who were accused of and tried for having committed war crimes were assured that they would not receive a death sentence. The British even agreed to give the Afrikaners £3 million (£ stands for the pound, British currency) to pay off the former republics' war debts. The British government also provided food and other necessities for the Afrikaners and recognized their property rights.

The treaty did not, however, provide as well for the blacks who were living in the republics. Lord Alfred Milner, the reform-minded British administrator involved in the negotiations, wanted very much for blacks living in southern Africa to have the right to vote. However, he did not dare insist that this right be included in the treaty. He feared it would cause Afrikaners and some British settlers to refuse to sign the treaty. In fact, the final surrender document stated outright that blacks would not be given the right to vote before self-government was established in the former republics.

The Unification of South Africa

At the time the treaty was signed, it was unclear what would happen next. Great Britain now had authority over four colonies in southern Africa. No one could tell whether they would eventually unite. If they did, it was unclear whether the British would order it or whether residents themselves would make it happen.

South Africa unified through a slow process that took from 1902 to 1910 to complete. One thing that helped push the colonies of South Africa toward unification was the election of a new government in Great Britain in 1906, which granted self-government to the Transvaal and the Orange River Colony. In May 1908, British and Afrikaners met at a conference, where they began to talk about making the four colonies into one independent country.

Another conference was held that winter. At it, representatives agreed that a single lawmaking authority should be established to rule all of South Africa. A constitution was drafted. After the colonies agreed to accept it, the British Parliament passed the South Africa Act, the law that made the several colonies of South Africa into one independent country. Formally named the Union of South Africa, it came into being in May 1910.

White South Africans rejoiced. For black South Africans, however, this was not a time of hope. In 1911 the total population of South Africa was six million. White people numbered 1.3 million. About two thirds of them were Afrikaners. There were four million blacks. The population also included half a million Coloured people and 200,000 Indians.

The Union Constitution spelled out a native policy. It had been approved by extremist Afrikaners, those who were most insistent that black South Africans be treated differently from white South Africans. The Constitution made sure the new country's society would be a segregated one. The Afrikaners had triumphed.

In the new country, laws made blacks inferior while white people enjoyed special privileges just because of their race. For example, only a few black people were allowed to vote. The former republics of Transvaal and the Orange Free State had allowed only white men to vote. This remained the same when they became provinces of South Africa. A

South Africa's Past

few blacks had been able to vote in Natal (economic criteria determined who could vote there). The Cape Colony's policy had been to allow anyone to vote as long as they could read and write and had a large income or owned a house and land outside of the blacks' reserves. These policies continued in South Africa. In the new country, only white men could serve in Parliament. In Natal and the Cape province, blacks were allowed to vote if they met the strict requirements, but few could do so. Over the decades that followed, segregation would increase. Laws said where black South Africans could live, what schools they could attend, and what jobs they could hold. They had little freedom.

After 1948, a new, stronger system of segregation, called apartheid, emerged. It imposed severe oppression on South Africans of color, but most especially black South Africans. Under apartheid, segregation was not only more rigid, but more strictly enforced. Apartheid lasted officially until 1994, when it was outlawed in a new South African Constitution. Nelson Mandela and others struggled for close to fifty years to overturn it.

CHAPTER 3

A Young Nelson Mandela

Blacks born in South Africa are members of tribes or clans. Many Americans know very little of their family's history. They may not even know when their ancestors arrived in the United States. But many black South Africans know a great deal about and are very proud of their heritage. All his life, the person who was born Rolihlahla Mandela, later know as Nelson, identified as a member of the Madiba clan and the Thembu tribe. The Thembu tribe speaks the Xhosa language and is considered part of a larger group, known as the Xhosa people. South Africans sometimes refer to Nelson Mandela as Madiba. This is a sign of respect because it refers to a powerful and courageous chief of long ago.

Childhood

Rolihlahla Mandela was born on July 18, 1918. The year of his birth was an important one in world history. It was the year World War I ended. The same year an influenza epidemic killed millions of people worldwide. At the time

A Young Nelson Mandela

Rolihlahla Mandela was born in his mother's village of Mvezo, which was a part of the Transkei territory, pictured here.

of his birth, the unified country of South Africa was very young. It had existed for only eight years.

Rolihlahla was named by his father, Gadla Henry Mphakanyiswa. The name he chose for his son translates into English as "pulling a branch off a tree." Some people say it means "troublemaker," while others translate it as "one who brings trouble on himself."[1]

His mother was Nonqaphi Nosekeni, also known as Fanny. In South Africa, tribesmen in the early twentieth century had several wives. Rolihlahla's mother was the third of four women Gadla Henry Mphakanyiswa married. Altogether his father had thirteen children: Rolihlahla was the youngest of his father's four sons and the first of his mother's four children.

Rolihlahla Mandela was born on his mother's homestead in a tiny village called Mvezo. Mvezo is located on the banks of the Mbashe River in the district of Umtata. Umtata is part of the Transkei territory. Rolihlahla lived there during his childhood. He saw his father only once in a while, because his father traveled between his wives' homesteads. They lived many miles apart. Nevertheless, Rolihlahla and his father were close: Black South African men were generally devoted fathers even when they did not live full-time with their children.[2]

When Rolihlahla was born, his father was a chief. The Thembu people had awarded him this status both because of his ancestry and because he had great intelligence and leadership skills.

For centuries, the native blacks of southern Africa had built their society around kings. Kings, however, did not hold absolute power. They took advice from clan heads or chiefs who ranked below them. As a clan chief, Rolihlahla's father was an extremely important counselor to two kings. Gadla Henry Mphakanyiswa could not read or write, but he knew his people's history and was a persuasive speaker. He played a very important part in government meetings.

At the time of Rolihlahla's birth, conditions were changing for black South Africans. Before the country united, they had held more political rights. After unification, however, the British government claimed the right to confirm all appointments of tribal authorities. The Union of South Africa soon began to follow a general native policy that hurt blacks and other people of color in other ways as well.

In 1911 the Mines and Works Act said that black South Africans could no longer work in skilled jobs without special permission from the government. They were forced to do hard labor, such as working in the mines and on the railroads. Blacks needed special permission to work at office jobs or in stores. In 1913 the Natives' Land Act said rural black South Africans could live on just 7.3 percent of the land designated as reserves for them.

These were the first of many laws passed to segregate South Africa. They took effect slowly. In 1923 the Urban Areas Act stated blacks had to leave their homes in cities. From that point on, blacks who lived in cities were supposed to live only in segregated communities on the cities' outskirts. They would be allowed to enter cities' centers only "to minister to the white man's need."[3]

Many black South Africans fought back against the segregation. Some white South Africans protested segregation, too. Mandela's father, Gadla Henry Mphakanyiswa, became militant. According to Mandela's memoirs, when he was still very young, his father received an order to appear before the local magistrate, a representative of the British government.

He sent back a message that said, "I will not come, I am still girding for battle."[4] In doing so, he was showing that he did not believe he needed to obey the laws of the British government. He followed the customs of his own people, instead. In response, the magistrate stripped Gadla Henry Mphakanyiswa of his position as chief in 1926. He no longer received a salary from the government. The government also took away most of his land and his animals. His entire family suffered from the loss of his fortune and title.

After Gadla Henry Mphakanyiswa was removed from office, Fanny, Rolihlahla's mother, and her children had to leave her homestead. She moved about twelve miles from Mvezo to Qunu, another very small village. In Qunu, she had friends and relations who could help support her children. Qunu is located in a grassy, well-watered valley. At that time, it had a population of a few hundred people. Everybody lived in a cluster of huts with mud walls and grass roofs.

In town, there were two small schools for little children and a general store. Outside of the village were fields, where women raised maize (corn) and pastures where cattle, sheep, goats, and horses grazed. Most of the year, the village's men were away, working on white men's farms or in mines. They usually returned twice a year to plow. Women and children hoed, weeded, and harvested the crops. The residents did not own their land. Almost no black South Africans owned their own property. The law required them to rent the land they farmed from the national government.

In Qunu, Rolihlahla's mother had three huts. She used one for storage, one for cooking, and one for sleeping. Nelson Mandela later remembered the huts always being crowded with children. He could not remember ever being alone. His extended family was extremely tight-knit. He spent as

A Young Nelson Mandela

By the time Rolihlahla Mandela was born, black South Africans were being shut out of skilled jobs and forced to go to work in the mines.

much time with his aunts and uncles as with his parents and thought of his cousins as brothers and sisters. When he was very young, he spent his days playing in the grass that surrounded his village. When he was five, he became a herd boy, tending calves and sheep.

Rolihlahla had time to swim and fish and to hunt birds with a slingshot. He learned how to gather food such as honey, fruit, and roots. He fought with sticks with his friends. The boys also played *thinti*—a game where one team uses sticks to try to knock down another team's target while defending its own.

At night, he went back to his mother's hut. While she cooked the evening meal, she told the children stories. Through these tales and observations, Mandela learned about his family tree and Xhosa customs, rituals, and taboos. (Taboos are a culture's banned behaviors. For example, most cultures consider it taboo to marry one's sister or brother.)

During his life at Qunu, Rolihlahla saw just a few white men. The local government official was white, as was the owner of the nearest store. Having learned from the actions of his elders, Rolihlahla later said, "I was aware that [whites] were to be treated with a mixture of fear and respect. But their role in my life was a distant one, and I thought little if at all about the white man in general or relations between my own people and these curious and remote figures."[5] In Qunu, Rolihlahla also met other blacks who were not part of the Xhosa people.

A New Name: Nelson

Rolihlahla's father followed the beliefs of his tribe's traditional religion, worshiping the god Qamata. His mother, on the other hand, met two brothers, members of another clan that also lived in the area, and heard them talk about their Christian faith. She converted to Christianity. She had Rolihlahla baptized as a Methodist.

At the age of seven, Rolihlahla was sent to a Christian school. He was the first member of his family ever to attend school. In those days, only one of about seven black South African children went to school.[6] Teachers at the school gave every black student a new English name. Thus on his first day there, his teacher gave him the name Nelson, by which white people would call him from then on. At this school, Nelson Mandela also started to learn English.

A Sad Loss

One night in 1927, when Rolihlahla was nine, his father arrived unexpectedly. He was making regular rounds of his wives' homes. But this time he came a few days earlier than expected.

When Rolihlahla realized that his father had arrived, he rushed to see him. He found his father lying down, in the middle of a terrible coughing fit. "Even to my young eyes, it was clear that my father was not long for this world. He was ill with some type of lung disease, but it was not diagnosed, as my father had never visited a doctor," Mandela later remembered.[7]

Gadla Henry Mphakanyiswa stayed with Rolihlahla and his mother for several days. He neither moved nor spoke. Finally, one night, he asked for his pipe. Within an hour, he died, with his pipe still lit.

Nelson Mandela later remembered that, after his father died, he felt "cut adrift," as though he had lost his anchor. His father had played a huge role in his life. "Although my mother was the center of my existence, I defined myself through my father," he later wrote.[8]

Sent Away

After a short time of mourning, Rolihlahla's mother decided that it was time for her son to leave Qunu. He never even asked where he would go or why he was being sent away. He was too stunned to protest. He and his mother set off on foot, carrying the few things he owned. They walked west all day. It was a hard trip. The dirt roads they walked on were rocky. Finally, late in the day, they arrived at Mqhekezweni, a village built around a large house, the fanciest he had ever seen. It was the royal residence of the regent, or king, Jongintaba Dalindyebo. Rolihlahla's father had been an advisor to Jongintaba.

About twenty tribal elders were sitting in the shade near the doorway of Jongintaba's main house. Suddenly, a car came in through the gate. Everybody jumped to their feet, shouting, "Hail, Jongintaba." Nelson Mandela always remembered the impression made by the man who stepped out. A short, heavy man, he wore an elegant suit and carried himself with confidence. Mandela desperately wanted to be part of Jongintaba's world. "Until then . . . ," he remembered, "I had no thought of money, or class, or fame, or power. Suddenly a new world opened before me."[9]

Later, Nelson Mandela found out why his mother had brought him there. When he had learned of Nelson's father's death, Jongintaba had offered to become Mandela's guardian. Mandela's mother agreed. Mandela essentially became an adopted or foster son to the king. Jongintaba and his wife, No England, acted as his parents. They advised him, scolded him, and cared for him.

After his father's death, Mandela went to live with Jongintaba Dalindyebo in the village of Mqhekezweni. This large tree stands in the middle of the compound where Mandela spent the rest of his childhood.

They also sent him to a new school. There, Mandela received a much better education than at the school in Qunu. He studied English and the Xhosa language, history, and geography. He worked very hard and did well.

Mandela also made new friends, especially with Jongintaba's children. Like them, in his spare time, he worked as a plowboy. Sometimes he herded animals or guided wagons. He rode horses and used slingshots to shoot birds.

In his new home, Mandela got to see a much more Westernized culture than he had in Qunu. The blacks in Mqhekezweni had more contact with whites. Now Mandela wore modern Western clothes. He went to the local Methodist church.

He also had a chance to watch his foster father at work. Periodically, the king presided over tribal meetings, where any man interested could come and debate an issue. Meetings ended only when the entire group had reached some kind of agreement. Looking back, Mandela believed he was watching true democracy at work.

He soon came to know his tribe's chiefs and headmen. At first, when they realized he was listening to them tell stories about Xhosa history, they shooed him away. But gradually, they came to accept and include him. In the end, Mandela was treated with respect by the men in his foster father's circle.

No Longer a Boy

At the age of sixteen, Mandela, his foster brother Justice, and twenty-five other boys took part in circumcision ritual ceremonies that signaled their entry into adulthood. Friends

A Young Nelson Mandela

and family gave the young men presents. Mandela received two cows and four sheep.

At first, it was a very happy day for him. However, his mood changed when he listened to the main ceremony speaker, who discussed blacks' treatment at the hands of white South Africans. Mandela remembered thinking at the time that the speaker was foolish. As a young man, Mandela still saw whites as benefactors. Later, he would develop very different opinions.

At this point, the boys were considered old enough to live away from home. Jongintaba sent Mandela away to school. His education was considered very important. When he grew up, his foster family planned for Mandela to become a counselor to Justice, Jongintaba's son, who would be the next king.

First, Mandela attended Clarkebury boarding school. Jongintaba himself drove Mandela to the school, which was run for black children by a white Methodist minister. It was a large place, with more than twenty buildings, all in the colonial or European style. There, Mandela took classes from teachers who had studied at a university. After classes, he worked in the principal's garden. At Clarkebury, Mandela finished in two years the full course of education that usually took three years.

In 1937 Mandela went on to a junior college at Healdtown, where he spent two years. Mandela, like his adopted father's other sons, received an exceptional education for a black child. Jongintaba took advantage of the few opportunities South Africa's segregated society would allow his children.

NELSON MANDELA and the END of APARTHEID

Mandela is seen here in a 1937 photograph. That year he started junior college, a rare opportunity for a black South African at that time.

A Young Nelson Mandela

University

After the young man completed his studies at Healdtown in 1939, Jongintaba decided Mandela should go on to the University College of Fort Hare. It was then the only residential college black South Africans were allowed to attend. To scholars from the United States or Europe, Fort Hare, with its enrollment of just one hundred fifty students, would have seemed very small. Its student body was made up mostly of blacks not just from South Africa but from elsewhere in Africa. There were also Asian students and people of mixed ancestry there. There were no white students.

While at Fort Hare, Mandela lived in a house owned by the Methodist church on the edge of campus. Never before had he seen so many modern conveniences, including flush toilets and hot showers. In his spare time, he attended church, played soccer, and ran for the cross-country team. He also enjoyed an active social life. He loved to dance, which made him popular with young women.[10]

In his first year of college, Mandela took classes in English, anthropology, politics, native administration, and a special type of law, Roman Dutch law. He did well in his studies, but he was not an outstanding student.

Right away, Mandela got involved in campus politics. He was elected to his dormitory's House Committee, whose members were usually older. At the same time, he became interested in world affairs. In 1939, when Mandela was twenty-one, South Africa joined World War II on the side of the Allies—Great Britain, France, the Soviet Union, and later, the United States—after Jan Christiaan Smuts, a South African Army general and long-time politician, became the country's prime minister. Every day, Mandela read about South African war efforts and developments in Europe and Japan.

When he first arrived at college, Nelson Mandela's goal was to work as an interpreter or clerk in the government's Native Affairs Department. All through his first year, this goal remained the same. Thinking about the future, he hoped to become part of South Africa's bureaucracy or government. He expected South African blacks' situation to remain in the future pretty much the same as it was then. What he and many others failed to realize was that the situation was about to change, and very quickly. Apartheid was about to begin. It would turn Mandela, the hopeful young college student, into an activist known throughout the world.

CHAPTER 4

The Rise of Apartheid

As a young man, Nelson Mandela witnessed a huge change in South Africa. He had grown up in racial segregation. It was not uncommon. In the first half of the twentieth century, segregation existed in many places in the world, including other African countries, Europe, Asia, the Caribbean, and the United States. In the United States, the civil rights movement won many rights for African Americans, but not until the 1960s.

The situation was very different in South Africa—it did not improve as the century progressed. In the years following the creation of South Africa in 1910, whites combined their power. The white population of South Africa remained divided into two separate groups: the English-speakers, who had originally come from Great Britain, and the Afrikaners, who were descended from South Africa's Dutch colonists. At first, most of the country's leaders were English-speakers. They played an important role in the South African economy, ruling the business world. Afrikaners generally worked in agriculture. Although it might be thought they would have less power, Afrikaners actually made up most of the voting

Well before apartheid was made an official policy, conditions for black South Africans were inferior to those of European descent. This shantytown near Johannesburg was home to many blacks in the 1940s.

body. Black South Africans, who made up the majority of the population, had virtually no power. They were legally oppressed and could not usually vote.

Political Background

The South African political party won the country's first general election, held in 1910. It was led by Louis Botha and Jan Christiaan Smuts, both of whom were Afrikaners. They both believed in coalition, saying that Afrikaners had to cooperate with English-speakers. They also accepted South Africa's membership in the British Empire.

Because of their views, many Afrikaners believed Botha and Smuts had sold out. Some became so upset that they no longer wanted Botha and Smuts as leaders. These Afrikaners formed a new political party, the National party, in 1914. Poor Afrikaners, as well as intellectuals, joined the Nationalists. They fought to protect Afrikaners' interests especially. They wanted South Africa to withdraw from the British Empire.

During World War I (1914–1918), some Afrikaners hoped to regain their independence from British rule. But the government put down their armed rebellion. South African soldiers also fought German troops in East Africa and South West Africa. After the war, mine owners wanted to replace some semiskilled white workers with blacks, whom they could pay much less. The white union went on strike and attacked police. The government finally settled the matter by declaring martial law (meaning for a short time the military controlled the government) and using weapons, including a tank and machine guns.

After this, Afrikaners were so angry that they refused to vote for Smuts's party. The Nationalists, led by J.B.M.

Hertzog, won the election of 1924. The new government passed more laws favoring whites in general and Afrikaners in particular. It also fought for autonomy, or less interference in its affairs, from Great Britain.

English and Dutch had been the official languages of the country. In 1925 Afrikaans replaced Dutch as an official language. By 1931 South Africa had begun to act on its own on the world scene. It had its own diplomats.

The Great Depression—a worldwide economic recession that caused terrible poverty and suffering—deeply hurt South Africa. With the economy in serious trouble, the two major political parties—Smuts's South African party and Hertzog's National Party—reached an agreement and together formed a coalition government. Members of both parties played important leadership roles. In 1934 the United party was created out of the combined South African and National Parties. Smaller political parties also formed. Now the Afrikaners, who believed strongly in preventing "mixing of the races," gained even more power.[1]

In 1939 trouble erupted for the new United Party. Great Britain had declared its intentions to fight Adolf Hitler's Nazi Germany in what would become World War II. Hertzog and his followers wanted South Africa to remain neutral during the war. Smuts and his followers, however, wanted to join the war on the side of Allies—Great Britain, France, the Soviet Union, and later, the United States. The South African Parliament finally voted to declare war on Germany, but by only a small margin. Hertzog demanded that the government be shut down and new elections held. The governor-general refused to let this happen. Hertzog then resigned as prime minister, and Smuts stepped back into the office.

The Rise of Apartheid

South African leader Jan Christiaan Smuts (right) sits next to British Prime Minister Winston Churchill. Smuts favored joining the Allies in fighting the Nazis in World War II and became a field marshal for the British army in 1941.

Black South Africans Suffer More and More

In the meantime, segregation continued to divide South African society. The Natives Land Act of 1913 had set aside as reserves less than 10% of the nation's land—just twenty-two million acres. This was declared enough land for black South Africans—80% of its society—to live on. The South African Native Trust was given authority to buy more land later. By 1939 reserves took up 11.7 percent of the total area of South Africa but it did not make much difference. The land the black South Africans were forced to live on was generally poor in quality, and very hard to farm.

Black South Africans' quality of life got only worse. As of 1925, black South African men had to pay a special tax called a poll tax if they wanted to vote. Eventually, black farming collapsed. Black South Africans could no longer feed themselves. Unable to support their families through farming the land they'd been assigned to, many men who lived on the reserves left. They got jobs working for white farms. Others took jobs in mines or industry.

By 1936 about a third of the total population of South Africa was black. The urban population of South Africa numbered three million. That means seventeen percent of black South Africans lived in towns.[2] Laws were written that dictated where blacks could live inside cities. To prevent more blacks from moving into the city, Parliament wrote "pass" laws. These laws forced blacks to get permission from the white farmers they worked for before they could quit, and also passes from government officials before they could look for work in a city. Laws also prevented black workers from striking and gave white workers the most skilled jobs.

The Rise of Apartheid

Fighting Back

The South African government made it very difficult for black South Africans to fight segregation. Blacks were armed to help South Africa in World War I but they had to return their weapons when the war ended. They also found very little support from Indian and Coloured South African minorities, who generally did not feel compelled to help black South Africans fight back against segregation. Although these ethnic groups also faced discrimination in South Africa, it was generally less severe than that against blacks.

Other problems that affected the black South African population was a breakdown in many families. Black families often fell apart when men were forced to leave the reserves to work. Traditional forms of black government also suffered—the young black men who left reserves to find work stopped seeing tribal leaders as authority figures.

Three political organizations were founded to try to improve the lives of those groups facing segregation in South Africa. Coloureds founded the African Political Organization, Indians formed the South African Indian Congress, and in 1912, blacks founded the South African Native National Congress. This last group would later be called the African National Congress (ANC).

The constitution of the ANC specifically stated that it would work within the law. It listed as its main concerns the "educational, social, economic and political elevation of the native people in South Africa."[3] The ANC's methods were cautious. It mostly protested upcoming laws by lobbying white political leaders.

From time to time, members of all three organizations cooperated. But whether together or apart, they failed to win any important victories. They were never able to get people united.

A more radical group, the Industrial and Commercial Worker Union (ICU), was formed in 1919. Protesting unfair conditions, ICU members refused to work, stole livestock, and destroyed property. Eventually, the group's leader was charged with stealing money from the ICU, and after much arguing between members, the group fell apart.[4] In 1921 white South Africans formed a Communist party, but it remained small.

Runaway

In 1940 Mandela returned to Fort Hare to complete his bachelor of arts degree. There he got in trouble with university authorities for supporting a student boycott. When he went home for vacation, he told his foster father, Jongintaba, that he was thinking about dropping out of school. His foster father insisted that he return. Mandela decided to let the matter rest for the time being.

A few weeks later, Jongintaba informed his family that he had arranged marriages for his son Justice and for Mandela. Neither young man wanted to get married. Rather than confront Jongintaba, they ran away together to Johannesburg. Mandela considered the city a place of great opportunity. The next day, the two men applied for jobs at the city's biggest gold mine. Justice got a good job as a clerk. Mandela became a mine policeman. When Jongintaba found out where they were, he tried to make them come home. They refused.

The Rise of Apartheid

Johannesburg in the 1940s. When Mandela moved to the city, he believed it was a place that offered great opportunities, despite the many restrictions placed on blacks.

Soon, Mandela changed jobs. He found a position as a clerk at a large law firm that handled business for both white and black South Africans. At night, he worked on correspondence lessons from the University of South Africa. He wanted to finish his degree and go on to study law.

As a law clerk, Mandela became friends with two Communists. Communist party members hoped that one day they would be able to overthrow the government. Mandela was just beginning to think about how his people might force the government to reform. Although Mandela did not join the Communist party, he often went to its meetings and parties. At the same time, Mandela learned a lot about the ANC.

Toward the end of 1941, Mandela saw his foster father, Jongintaba, who expressed approval of Mandela's plans to study law. They parted on good terms.

In August of 1942, Jongintaba died. After his funeral, Mandela returned to Johannesburg alone because Justice had taken his father's place, serving as the new king.

At the end of 1942, Mandela finished his college studies, earning a bachelor's degree. He continued to work for the law firm and he started taking courses part-time at the University of Witwatersrand in Johannesburg, working toward a law degree. At the time, he was the only black student in the law school.[5]

By this time, Mandela was spending a lot of time with Gaur Radebe, the only other black staff member at his law firm. Radebe took him to meetings of the ANC, and he helped him adopt a PanAfrican point of view. PanAfricans believed that, ultimately, all black South Africans, regardless of what tribe or clan they had been born into, should unite to fight for reform. During this period, Mandela also met Walter

The Rise of Apartheid

Sisulu, a leader of the ANC who would have even more influence on him than Radebe.

At this time, the ANC was setting new goals. In 1941 British Prime Minister Winston Churchill and United States President Franklin Delano Roosevelt had signed the Atlantic Charter, which supported the rights of all individuals. Africans had been inspired by the charter. Members of the ANC had written their own charter, which they called the African Claims. It demanded full citizenship for all Africans. It also called for blacks to be allowed to own land in South Africa.[6]

More and More Radical

In 1943 Mandela often went to Sisulu's house, where ANC members gathered to visit and talk about politics and their cause. Decades later, Sisulu would remember, "When a young man of Nelson's nature came, it was a godsend to me. Because we were looking for people who could finally have influence on the situation in the country."[7] Mandela was intelligent and self-confident, and he would prove himself dedicated.

Mandela became so involved with Sisulu's ANC group that he became a member of a delegation of young men that went to meet with ANC president Dr. Alfred B. Xuma. They wanted to establish a Youth League for the ANC. They had already drafted a constitution and written a manifesto, outlining specific actions they wanted to take. Xuma protested, arguing that a youth league should recruit for the ANC and take no action on its own.

Still, Mandela and his friends proceeded with their plans. After the meeting with Xuma, a provisional committee of the Youth League formed. Its members attended the ANC

NELSON MANDELA and the END of APARTHEID

Walter Sisulu was a leader of the African National Congress (ANC) and encouraged Mandela to get involved in the fight for equality.

The Rise of Apartheid

National Congress in December 1943. The ANC accepted the proposal for forming the youth group.

The Youth League began on Easter Sunday in 1944. One hundred young black men attended its first meeting. That day, the members elected officers. Mandela was elected to the executive committee.

The Youth League members were dedicated to African nationalism. They wanted to unite the various black tribes living in South Africa and overthrow the white government. Eventually, Sisulu and Mandela, in particular, hoped the Youth League would be able to gain control of the entire ANC, forcing it to become a much more radical organization than in the past.[8]

CHAPTER 5

Apartheid—"Apartness"

Apartheid is an Afrikaner word that means "apartness." In 1948 the National Party came into power in South Africa. Nationalists began to pass laws that created a new system of rigid segregation called apartheid. It forced all nonwhites to live apart from whites.

Apartheid officially began in 1948. Its roots stemmed from the decision Dutch and British officials had made years earlier to keep native Africans, slaves, and Coloured people from having a voice in the colonial government. In the years that followed, the white settlers and their descendants kept control of the government, despite the fact that they made up a minority of South Africa's population.

The segregated history of South Africa made it easy for the National Party to establish apartheid as a new official government policy. Most blacks already were not allowed to vote. Supporters of apartheid wanted complete racial segregation. They did not, however, want nonwhites to enjoy rights equal to those of whites under a so-called "separate but equal" policy like that of the United States. Instead, they pushed for a society "in which the lighter your skin, the more benefits you received."[1]

Those who pushed for apartheid recognized four categories in society: white, Indian, Coloured, and African, or black. Whites generally enjoyed comfortable lives. The government gave them excellent public services, including schools, hospitals, parks, transportation, water, electricity, and sewage. Nonwhites did not get the same public services. Indian and Coloured people were also mistreated, but blacks were always the most deprived.

Once in power, the Nationalists began to make laws to extend the anti-black customs and traditions that were already in place. The government's goal became "to preserve white power in general—and Afrikaner power in particular."[2] A great deal of social upheaval followed.

Primary Source: The National Party's Colour Policy—March 29, 1948

[Apartheid's] aim is the maintenance and protection of the European population of the country as a pure White race, the maintenance and protection of the indigenous racial groups as separate communities, with prospects of developing into self-supporting communities within their own areas, and the stimulation of national pride, self-respect, and mutual respect among the various races of the country.[3]

The Nationalist government moved quickly to repress nonwhite people. It banned mixed marriages—marriages between whites and nonwhites.

The South African legislature also passed laws that removed anyone who was not an Afrikaner from a position of authority in the government. New laws required all employees in government offices to be able to speak both English and Afrikaans. This meant that not only blacks and other nonwhites but also many white English speakers were forced out of their jobs. Afrikaners who could speak English, as well as their native Afrikaans, got the jobs instead.

Soon the Nationalist government required every resident of South Africa to be issued an identification card that recorded his or her race. To decide what race a particular person was, officials often used ridiculous measures. For instance, they might push a pencil into a person's hair. If the pencil stayed in, the person would be classified as black and restricted accordingly.[4] New laws required people to live within their racial category. This meant that many people had to move. Laws allowed the government to take the land and property of more than three million people.

By 1953 South African law would provide for separate facilities—including post offices, trains, offices, beaches, parks, bus stops, benches, service counters, and elevators—for whites and nonwhites. The lives of all nonwhite South Africans were terribly disrupted by laws that told them where to live and work.

Life Under Apartheid

Apartheid meant that Nelson Mandela, like other blacks and nonwhites, had to give up many of his hopes and dreams. When he first went to college, black South Africans were still

Apartheid—"Apartness"

Apartheid affected all South Africans, young and old. Here, a group of white children wade in a pond that is marked "For European Children Only."

allowed to work for the government. Apartheid now meant that he faced limits both in how he could earn his living and the type of life he could lead.

In the 1940s, Mandela experienced huge changes in his personal life. He moved from place to place. Several times he lived for weeks or months with Walter Sisulu's family. At his house, he met Sisulu's cousin, Evelyn Mase, who was training to become a nurse and also came from Transkei.

In 1944 Nelson Mandela and Evelyn Mase were married. At first, they lived with her family. In 1946 they had their first child, a son named Madiba Thembekile. Because they had a child, the state let them have a house of their own. It was a tiny house with just two rooms. It was in Orlando West. The neighborhood was filled with hundreds of houses just like theirs. They all had tin roofs and cement floors. None had a flush toilet. A double bed filled up the entire bedroom. There was no electricity in the neighborhood, so they used kerosene lamps.

For years, Mandela had frequently lived with friends and relations. Now his own house was always filled with visitors. According to the customs of his tribe, all members of his large extended family could expect a welcome. His sister moved in with them so she could attend a local high school.

Nelson Mandela greatly enjoyed family life, but his devotion to his political causes meant he was rarely at home. For the first year of his marriage, he continued to work. In 1947 he left the law firm of Witkin, Sidelsky, and Eidelman to study law full-time at the University of the Witwatersrand. Without a salary, he had to take out a loan from the Bantu Welfare Trust at the South African Institute of Race Relations.

Apartheid—"Apartness"

At that time, Evelyn was working as a nurse. His loan and her salary combined to make enough for the family to live on. Three months later, however, Mandela had to borrow more money because Evelyn was about to go on maternity leave. Their second child was a girl named Makaziwe. From her birth, she was sickly. Her parents took turns staying up with her at night. But despite their many efforts and Evelyn's training, the baby did not get well. Makaziwe died before she was a year old.

Protest

From the beginning, many South Africans were against apartheid. White South African churches issued statements against the new system. English-speaking students at white universities opposed apartheid. White women formed a protest group called the Black Sash. The Communist party tried to take away power from the Nationalists. The ANC's Youth League was the most vocal protest group.

Mandela remained very involved with the ANC Youth League after his marriage. In 1947 he served on the executive committee of the Transvaal branch of the ANC. In 1948 he served as the Youth League's general secretary.

When apartheid was instituted, Mandela was "stunned and dismayed."[5] One of his friends thought the Nationalists' rise to power would, in the end, help South African blacks. Now he hoped they would unite to fight their common enemy. Members of the Youth League became extremely revolutionary. The Youth League issued a call for civil disobedience, a form of peaceful protest which means that individuals refuse to follow certain laws in an effort to influence a change in government policy. The League's struggle against the government would last for more than twelve years. By the end of 1949, members of the Youth League had already influenced the ANC as a whole, getting the national conference to endorse a program of action designed to oppose white rule. Under this plan, blacks would refuse to go along with the white government.

In May 1950, the government decided to outlaw the Communist party. The Communists staged a mass labor strike, in protest. Mandela was against black participation in the strike because it had not been planned by the ANC. He wanted blacks to continue to go to work. However, black South African workers did go out on strike in force. The day ended in disaster when policemen opened fire on a crowd of black protesters, killing eighteen.[6]

The government then drafted a new law called the Suppression of Communism Act. Under it, any person who tried to bring about change through unlawful acts could be considered a Communist. The law banned almost all political protest.

A number of groups, including the ANC, took part in the National Day of Protest on June 26, 1950. Eventually, the alliance forged between the ANC and the Communist party would cause problems within the ANC.

Mandela's participation in anti-apartheid activity was limited by his new job at a law firm. Mandela had to make the tough choice as to which would come first—his politics or his family. Devoted to his beliefs, Mandela continued to put politics ahead of his family. In fact, Mandela worked so hard that he had little time to celebrate the birth of his second son, Makgatho Lewanika. His commitment to politics was becoming all-consuming.

In 1951 Mandela became president of the Youth League. He saw his greatest challenge as maintaining contact between

Apartheid—"Apartness"

In the 1950s, black South Africans were growing increasingly frustrated with their unfair treatment by the government. Here, a crowd marches to protest the injustices of apartheid.

the Youth League and the people. In 1952 he was elected president of a branch of the African National Congress—the Transvaal branch, with headquarters in Johannesburg. Mandela was one of four ANC deputy presidents.

At this time, the ANC was going through important changes. In the early days of the ANC, its president, Pixley Seme, had, along with others, insisted that the group remain nonviolent. Seme had been succeeded as president by Alfred Xuma. Xuma had done a lot to strengthen the ANC. Under him, the ANC Youth League had formed. Still, he had continued to stress the need for moderation. He thought that, if the organization acted too early, before the masses of South African people were ready to take part, the government would simply persecute ANC leaders, who would then be unable to get anything done.

CHAPTER 6

Fighting Back

In the early 1950s, ANC leaders disagreed as to how to fight back against apartheid. Older ANC leaders were committed to moderation. Young ANC leaders like Mandela, Walter Sisulu, and Oliver Tambo, on the other hand, were willing to risk everything to try to bring about change. They did not want to wait to try to negotiate with the government. They were impatient to act.

In 1949 the young leaders pushed ANC President Alfred Xuma out of office by convincing other ANC members not to reelect him. His successor, James Moroka, was elected with their backing. In return, he gave them much more power in the organization. Under their influence, the ANC became committed to what its authors called the Programme of Action, a program of "militant" resistance.[1]

The first important step the ANC made under Moroka was to begin to cooperate with the South African Indian Congress (SAIC) and other South Africans who were also fighting apartheid. In 1952 the ANC and the Indian Congress formed the Joint Planning Council. It launched a defiance campaign against the government.

First, Moroka and Walter Sisulu wrote to South African Prime Minister Daniel Malan, asking him to repeal the new discriminatory laws. They said that their people desired "democracy, liberty, and harmony" and were "fully resolved to achieve them in our lifetime."[2] Malan replied that the government would not back down and warned that, if troublemakers continued to resist government efforts to segregate South African society, the government would "use the full machinery at its disposal to quell any disturbances."[3]

The ANC decided it was not afraid of Malan's threats, and in conjunction with the Indian Congress, began its Campaign for the Defiance of Unjust Laws. Mandela served as volunteer-in-chief for the campaign. This assignment meant he coordinated the efforts of thousands of those who refused to accept apartheid, finding ways for them to defy the government and scheduling demonstrations.

Some Coloureds joined the campaign. Many of them spoke Afrikaans and had been raised as Afrikaners during the period of less extreme segregation. Conditions had significantly worsened for them when apartheid began. Other Coloureds, however, supported the Nationalists.

Following Mandela's instructions, on June 26, 1952, thousands risked prison terms. Blacks and Indians sat on "white only" benches in parks. They broke government-imposed curfews. In businesses and offices, they went up to desks that were supposed to serve only whites. A white sympathizer broke the law by entering a black township without permission.

Protesters continued their acts of defiance into December of 1952. Eventually, the government arrested some eight thousand participants in the campaign.

Fighting Back

South African Prime Minister Daniel Malan rejected the ANC's request to repeal new apartheid laws.

In October 1952, the nature of the campaign changed. Violence broke out among protesters for the first time. Both blacks and whites rioted, protesting the violence. Police broke up these protests with force. On November 10, police stormed a prayer meeting sponsored by the ANC, despite the fact that its organizers had permission from police to hold the meeting. Policemen fixed bayonets to the ends of their rifles and charged at those who had gathered to pray together for the end of apartheid.

The ANC finally stopped the defiance campaign because the government had significantly cracked down, treating those arrested harshly. In one way, the campaign had cost its supporters dearly. Fourteen protesters had died and another thirty-five were wounded at the hands of police.

On the other hand, the ANC had succeeded. By the end of the campaign, its membership had swelled from seven thousand to one hundred thousand—the Congress had ninety-three thousand new dues-paying members. In addition, more than eight thousand of its members had been arrested, bringing attention to the wrong being done to black South Africans.[4]

Criminal Charges

In the middle of the campaign, on July 30, 1952, twenty-one ANC leaders were arrested, including Mandela. After being released on bail, they went back to work on the campaign. They all went on trial in September.

The public held rallies in the street to demonstrate support for them. During the trial, the ANC president hired his own attorney and publicly denounced the cause.

In December, the judge found every defendant guilty. He sentenced them to nine months of imprisonment at hard

Fighting Back

labor but suspended the sentence for two years. In his closing statements, the judge said that, while they had broken the law, he regarded them as examples of nonviolence.

During this period, Mandela made a bold professional move. He opened his own law office in August 1952. He became partners with Oliver Tambo, whom he had known since his days at Fort Hare and who was also involved in the ANC.

Theirs was the only all-black firm then in South Africa. Often they represented blacks who had been arrested for breaking apartheid laws. They themselves were breaking the law by keeping their office in the city.

New Protest Methods

After the defiance campaign trial, ANC leaders were harassed by police and government officials. The government said they could not attend political meetings. If they did so, they would be arrested. Forbidden to call mass meetings, issue press statements, or publish leaflets, ANC leaders had to come up with new ways to stir people to action.

One new protest method they used was a boycott of black schools. Recently, the government had created the new Bantu education system. No longer could black children go to schools run by churches or missionaries. Mandela and other ANC leaders believed the new public education was so inferior that they asked black families not to let their children go to the schools the government ran for black children.

In September 1953, the government ordered Mandela to give up his place in the ANC. Working from behind the scenes, he helped organize the Congress of the People. Members of the ANC, the South African Indian Congress, the

NELSON MANDELA and the END of APARTHEID

Mandela strikes a fighting pose in 1952, the year that he opened up the only all-black law firm in South Africa.

Fighting Back

South African Coloured People's Organization, the Congress of Democrats (a group of antigovernment whites), and the South African Congress of Trade Unions sent three thousand delegates to the congress. It issued a document called the Freedom Charter. It was moderate in tone, including little more than statements such as, "All shall be equal before the law!" The government considered it very subversive.[5]

Treason!

On December 5, 1956, the government ordered 156 people, including Nelson Mandela, arrested and charged with high treason. The trial would last for more than four years. During that period, Mandela and his codefendants were free on bail. They went about their daily lives, but had the threat of eventual imprisonment always over their heads.

During this period, Mandela and his wife, Evelyn, grew apart because he devoted so little time to his family. They divorced in 1957. In the meantime, Mandela started a new romance with Winnie Nomzano Madikizela, a social worker. She understood from the beginning that they could never lead an ordinary life. Mandela would always spend most of his time fighting apartheid. They married on June 14, 1958.

In the late 1950s, the ANC split. Some African nationalists had been complaining that the ANC was not doing enough to fight apartheid. This was largely because many of the ANC's more radical leaders were in prison.

On April 6, 1959, three hundred former members of the ANC, led by Robert Mangaliso Sobukwe, founded a new group. It was called the Pan-Africanist Congress (PAC). The PAC launched its own anti-apartheid campaign.

NELSON MANDELA and the END of APARTHEID

The defendants of the 1956 treason trial included 156 members of the ANC. Mandela is in the third row, eighth from the right.

Fighting Back

Police Open Fire at Sharpeville

On March 21, 1960, answering a call by the PAC, fifteen thousand blacks gathered at Sharpeville. They protested pass laws by going out without their passes. Police opened fire on the protesters. Sixty-seven of them died. Close to two hundred were wounded.

The world reacted with horror to the news of the massacre of protesters. Political leaders in the United Nations and from around the globe began to pressure the South African government to abolish apartheid.

In the aftermath of Sharpeville, the black South African population showed extreme anger. Mandela and other members of the ANC stayed up all night, discussing how to respond.

On March 26, the president of the ANC, Albert Luthuli, publicly burned the pass the government required him, like all other blacks, to carry. Two days later, as part of a Day of Mourning led by the ANC, Mandela and Duma Nokwe burned their passes at a meeting attended by hundreds of people and recorded by dozens of photographers.

Martial Law

At the same time, the ANC also began to put together a very successful protest strike. To get people to return to work, police hunted down strikers at their homes and beat them. The government had to declare a state of emergency (in a state of emergency governments typically forego regular procedures, devoting their attention to trying to reestablish control). It outlawed both the PAC and the ANC and established martial law.

NELSON MANDELA and the END of APARTHEID

Nelson and Winnie Mandela pose for a photo on their wedding day in 1957.

Fighting Back

Both the ANC and the PAC sent some leaders out of the country so that they could continue the fight against apartheid in exile. Oliver Tambo fled to Zambia and took control of the ANC from outside.

Back in South Africa, thousands of strikers and other protesters were arrested on political charges. On March 30, Mandela was arrested because of his continuing involvement with the ANC. Other political leaders were arrested, too.

On Trial

Soon the political prisoners were moved to a jail in Pretoria. They stayed there until the government lifted its state of emergency in August. By that time, their trial had already begun. The defendants used what has since been called the "Mandela defense." Asked whether they wanted to plead guilty or not guilty, they would respond not guilty, but they would state it in a special way. All of them said something like this: "It is this government which is guilty, M'Lord. I plead not guilty."[6] The state's prosecutors were trying to prove that Mandela and the others were Communists who advocated violence. But they did not prove their case. On March 29, 1961, Mandela and the other defendants in the Treason Trial were found not guilty. The judge found that, while leaders of the ANC had occasionally called for members to resort to violence to bring about change, the organization did not have an official policy calling for the violent overthrow of the government.[7]

In March 1961, just as his trial was ending, Nelson Mandela appeared as the key speaker at the All-in Africa Conference in Pietermaritzburg. The government orders banning him from attending such meetings had expired. Still, Mandela knew that he would be in danger if he

NELSON MANDELA and the END of APARTHEID

Victims lie on the ground in the aftermath of the 1960 Sharpeville shootings. Violence broke out during an anti-apartheid event in which protesters were encouraged to leave their passes at home.

Fighting Back

Primary Source: Recollections of Sharpeville

We heard the chatter of machine guns, then another, than another. Bodies were falling. Hundreds of children were running. Some of the children were shot, too. Still the shooting went on.

The police have claimed they were in desperate danger because the crowd was stoning them. Yet only three policemen were reported to have been hit by stones—and more than 200 Africans were shot down. The police also have said that the crowd was armed with "ferocious weapons," which littered the compound after they fled.

I saw no weapons, although I looked very carefully, and afterwards studied the photographs of the death scene. While I was there I saw only shoes, hats and a few bicycles left among the bodies. The crowd gave me no reason to feel scared, though I moved among them without any distinguishing mark to protect me, quite obvious with my white skin. I think the police were scared though, and I think the crowd knew it.[8]

> –Humphrey Tyler was the only journalist at Sharpeville when police opened fire on protestors. These are his memories of the scene.

continued to defy the government publicly. Therefore, at the conference, he announced he was soon going to go underground. In the months that followed his appearance at the All-In Africa Conference of March 1961, the South African police tried and failed to capture Nelson Mandela. He used different disguises and lived on the run.

CHAPTER 7

Arrested and Imprisoned

While on the run, Nelson Mandela became invested in a different sort of protest. By this time, some black leaders fighting apartheid in South Africa had decided that nonviolence was not working. Peaceful protests seemed unlikely to bring an end to apartheid. So members of ANC, including Mandela, founded a new underground wing of the ANC called *Umkhonto we Sizwe* (Spear of the Nation). Its goal was to sabotage government works. "The symbol of the spear was chosen because with this simple weapon Africans had resisted the incursions of whites for centuries," Mandela explained.[1]

As a member of Umkhonto we Sizwe, Nelson Mandela organized a guerrilla army of volunteers. On December 16, 1961, Umkhonto we Sizwe leaders bombed power plants and government buildings. Umkhonto we Sizwe, together with the militant wing of the Pan-African Conference and the African Resistance Movement, would undertake two hundred such actions before the government finally shut them down.[2]

NELSON MANDELA and the END of APARTHEID

In 1961 Mandela was forced to go into hiding. He was wanted by the government for having defied orders against participating in anti-apartheid organizations.

Arrested and Imprisoned

In the winter of 1961, Mandela was living on a farm in Rivonia, a suburb of Johannesburg. Other political activists who were in trouble with the government also hid out there. Occasionally, Winnie and his children sneaked in to see him.

Sometimes he put on one of his disguises and left South Africa to go elsewhere in African countries to gain support for the anti-apartheid cause. When he heard on the radio that Albert Luthuli, president of the ANC, had received the Nobel Peace Prize, he was happy for his friend and glad to know that the cause was gaining world recognition.

In February 1962, Mandela attended a meeting of what would later be called the Organization of African Unity. Its goal was to support liberation movements all over the African continent. At the meeting, he was promised support for the ANC and Umkhonto we Sizwe.

After visiting other countries, including England, where he received more promises of support, Mandela returned to South Africa. He continued to work underground to end apartheid.

Captured

On August 5, 1962, Mandela was captured. He was returning from a secret political activists' meeting to the farm in Rivonia with Cecil Williams, a white theater director who also belonged to Umkhonto we Sizwe. To avoid attracting attention, Mandela was driving their car while Williams rode in the back. They were pretending that Mandela was Williams's chauffeur. But an informer had told the police to watch for them, and they were stopped. Mandela and Williams were both arrested.

Tried on charges of inciting workers to strike and leaving the country illegally, Mandela received a prison sentence of

Primary Source: Umkhonto we Sizwe: We Are at War!

Why we fight

To you, the sons and daughters of the soil, our case is clear.

The white oppressors have stolen our land. They have destroyed our families. They have taken for themselves the best that there is in our rich country and have left us the worst. They have the fruits and the riches. We have the backbreaking toil and the poverty.

We burrow into the belly of the earth to dig out gold, diamonds, coal, uranium. The white oppressors and foreign investors grab all this wealth. It is used for their enrichment and to buy arms to suppress and kill us.

In the factories, on the farms, on the railways, wherever you go, the hard, dirty, dangerous, badly paid jobs are ours. The best jobs are for whites only.

In our own land we have to carry passes; we are restricted and banished while the white oppressors move about freely.

Our homes are hovels; those of the whites are luxury mansions, flats and farmsteads.

There are not enough schools for our children; the standard of education is low, and we have to pay for it. But the government uses our taxes and the wealth we create to provide free education for white children.

We have suffered long enough.

Over 300 years ago the white invaders began a ceaseless war of aggression against us, murdered our forefathers, stole our land and enslaved our people.

Today they still rule by force. They murder our people. They still enslave us.

Only by meeting force with force can we win back our motherland.

> –The militant wing of the ANC, Umkhonto we Sizwe, was set up by those who believed only violence could counter violence.[3]

Arrested and Imprisoned

five years. At first, he was housed in Pretoria Central prison. Conditions were terrible. Black prisoners were clothed in just a shirt, shorts, and sandals year-round. Later, he was transferred to Robben Island, a maximum-security prison.

At Pretoria, Mandela had been one of seven political prisoners. On Robben Island, there were many more. Life was hard. The prisoners were forced to perform manual labor, pounding stones into gravel.

The worst thing about prison life for Mandela was his lack of contact with the outside world. He was not able to have visitors, receive letters, or read newspapers. He was allowed to spend time with other prisoners, whom he often encouraged. He taught some to read and write. He himself wrote a great deal, even though he was allowed to receive and send only one letter every six months. Every once in a while, on the few occasions when a political prisoner was released, he could get a message out. His living arrangements remained horrible. His bed was the floor. In May 1963, his wife, Winnie, was charged with violating her political ban by attending political gatherings. Her trial started in September.

On July 12, police made a sweep, arresting many other dissidents at Rivonia. Following the arrests, the government brought new charges against Nelson Mandela. Mandela and nine codefendants were charged with 199 acts of violence. Their attorney pointed out that Mandela had been in prison on the dates when 156 of the acts occurred. The judge threw out the indictment, but the state brought another.

The government began to boast that the PAC was no longer any threat. More than three thousand people accused of belonging to the PAC had been arrested. By December 1963, forty political prisoners had been sentenced to death.

NELSON MANDELA and the END of APARTHEID

Mandela spent eighteen years in the prison on Robben Island. This photo shows the cell where he lived.

Arrested and Imprisoned

Another thousand had received prison sentences of one to twenty-five years.

On June 12, 1964, the verdict was handed down: Nelson Mandela and seven of the other defendants received life sentences. Because they had thought they might get the death penalty, they reacted to the news with joy. None of the defendants believed he would actually be in prison for life. Eventually, the prisoners expected, their imprisonment would come to embarrass the South African government, which would be forced to release them. Many members of the public gathered outside Pretoria's Palace of Justice to hear the verdict. When Winnie Mandela and Nelson Mandela's mother appeared on the steps, the crowd cheered. After the trial, the defendants were taken to Robben Island.

The World Pays Attention

The government brought the first round of anti-apartheid violence to an end. By using force and making many arrests, it was able to break up Umkhonto we Sizwe, Poqo (the militant wing of the PAC), and the African Resistance Movement. But even when Mandela and the other anti-apartheid leaders were convicted in 1964, the resistance movement did not fall apart.

In the decade that followed, many books appeared overseas about the situation in South Africa. At the same time, the South African economy boomed. Blacks began to get more semiskilled jobs. They began to fight for fair wages and equal treatment at work.

One very important thing in the anti-apartheid struggle happened while Mandela and other leaders were in prison. A new generation of black South Africans became involved in the movement. In 1968 a college student named

Primary Source: Speech by Nelson Mandela

This then is what the ANC is fighting. Their struggle is a truly national one. It is a struggle of the African people, inspired by their own suffering and their own experience. It is a struggle for the right to live. During my lifetime I have dedicated myself to this struggle of the African people. I have fought against white domination, and I have fought against black domination. I have cherished the ideal of a democratic and free society in which all persons live together in harmony and with equal opportunities. It is an ideal which I hope to live for and to achieve. But if needs be, it is an ideal for which I am prepared to die.

This is from the speech delivered by Nelson Mandela on April 20, 1964, at the beginning of his trial. [4]

Arrested and Imprisoned

Steve Biko left a white group called the National Union of South African Students and formed the new South African Students' Organization. His statements and writings would lead to a rise in "black consciousness." Biko wrote:

> Black consciousness is in essence the realisation by the black man of the need to rally together with his brothers around the cause of their subjection—the blackness of their skin—and to operate as a group in order to rid themselves of the shackles that bind them to perpetual servitude.[5]

As time passed, more and more foreign nations began to criticize South Africa for its system of apartheid. Other former British colonies had become independent since the creation of South Africa. Black nationalists, rather than white settlers, controlled the new nations of Ghana, Sierra Leone, Nigeria, and the Gambia.

In 1960 British Prime Minister Harold Macmillan warned the South African Parliament that Great Britain could not support South Africa if it continued to repress black nationalism. In 1961 South Africa became a republic and formally left the British Empire. By 1965 Great Britain had transferred power to black nationalists in its former territories of Tanzania, Uganda, Kenya, Malawi, and Zambia. When South Africa was first formed, Great Britain had intended to allow it eventually to take over the territories of Lesotho, Botswana, and Swaziland. Instead, Great Britain granted those territories independence.

From 1952 on, the United Nations (UN) passed annual resolutions against apartheid. After 1967, it published many publications exposing South Africa's racial policies. It called apartheid "a crime against humanity."[6]

The South African government tried to win support from other world leaders by claiming to be a stable, civilized country that was fighting Communism. For a long time, many American and European investors continued to trade with South Africa. The United States remained South Africa's main trading partner through the 1970s. The South African economy depended on a lot of foreign money. However, human rights protesters complained strongly to companies that invested in South Africa. Gradually, those companies felt pressure to cut off trade, which many did.

In 1973 the government offered to let Mandela go if he agreed to return to Transkei, the isolated region where he had been born. He refused. He would not agree to be released if the government would not let him move about freely or speak in public. Despite the fact that he was behind bars, he was famous and influential, by that time the most important black leader in South Africa.

In 1979 the country of India celebrated Mandela's achievements by giving him the Nehru prize for peace. In 1981 several United States congressmen tried to see him, but the South African government would not let them. Seventeen thousand Frenchmen signed a petition calling for Mandela's release, which was sent to the South African Embassy in France.[7] Members of the resistance movement in South Africa looked to Mandela for inspiration. He became a symbol for people all over the globe who were fighting for human rights.

In 1982 Mandela was transferred to Pollsmoor Prison, located on the South African mainland, near Cape Town. By the mid-1980s, the South African government was constantly

Arrested and Imprisoned

As the years passed, international awareness of apartheid grew and more people demanded change in South Africa. This anti-apartheid march took place in England in 1969.

under pressure from protesters within and abroad to reform, and to release Mandela. He was the most important political prisoner in the world.

The government wanted to free him, but realized it had to be done in a public, symbolic way. It began to negotiate with Mandela concerning his release. Mandela, however, would not accept the government's terms. He remained so dedicated to the overthrow of apartheid that he gave up his freedom for the cause. He would not allow his release to bring his freedom alone. He demanded to remain in prison until all blacks and other people of color in South Africa could be free from the system of apartheid.

CHAPTER 8

Freedom for Mandela and His People

In the 1970s and 1980s, Pieter Willem Botha was first prime minister and then president of South Africa. He came to believe it was time to end apartheid.

Botha's interest in changing the apartheid system did not come from any moral convictions, or because he thought it was wrong or unfair. Instead, he was worried about international efforts to overturn the system. More and more, other countries were taking a stand against apartheid through methods like economic sanctions (not trading with South Africa) and sports boycotts (athletes would not travel to that country). The government tried bringing in Coloured and Indian citizens, seating them in their own houses in Parliament. But attempts to create a South African middle class did not mean that the government planned to grant blacks and other groups equal rights.

In fact, Botha's government continued to oppress blacks. In response, anti-apartheid protesters began to stage new, often violent, protests. On June 16, 1976, thousands of black schoolchildren who did not want to be taught in Afrikaans, as the law demanded, held a huge demonstration in Soweto.

NELSON MANDELA and the END of APARTHEID

Pieter Willem Botha, leader of South Africa during much of the apartheid era, moved to change the system largely because of how the international community's disdain was affecting the country.

Freedom for Mandela and His People

The police were called in to break up their protest. The police resorted to violence, picking up guns and using tear gas to break up the crowd. A thirteen-year-old child was shot and killed.[1]

In the months that followed, the South African government continued to use harsh measures to put down other uprisings. South African police and soldiers killed 575 people, including 494 Africans, seventy-five Coloureds, five whites, and one Indian.[2] During the Botha administration, a secret police force brutalized both anti-apartheid activists and those suspected of working toward reform in general. In 1977 the government banned Steve Biko's South African Students' Organization. The government also ordered the arrest of those blacks identified as leaders of the resistance movement (who were not already in jail). Biko, the leader of a new generation of resistance fighters, was among those arrested. He died while in police custody, of injuries to his head. The news of his death shocked human rights activists in and out of South Africa.

Faced with real danger, thousands of militant blacks fled South Africa. They did not leave to find somewhere new to live in peace. Instead, they went to military training camps. The ANC and PAC, although officially banned, still existed. Their members just worked in secrecy. These groups set up military training camps in Tanzania and Angola, where South African blacks were trained in guerrilla tactics. Sneaking back into South Africa, they unleashed a new wave of violence. At the same time, the government went to great lengths to keep white South Africans from learning about atrocities against nonwhites.

NELSON MANDELA and the END of APARTHEID

Throughout the 1970s, anti-apartheid protests continued in South Africa. The Soweto Uprising of 1976, pictured here, became violent when police attacked young people calling for better education.

Deals Are Offered

Several times during Botha's administration, officials approached Mandela to discuss his possible release. In 1987 the government approached him with what he later described as "its first concrete proposal."[3] Mandela, however, would never have considered a deal that would force him to leave the country, keep his mouth shut, or stop fighting against apartheid.

His refusal to take a deal and walk away free would cost Mandela dearly. In 1988, soon after he had turned seventy, Nelson Mandela became sick with tuberculosis. Winnie and his daughter were allowed to come see him in the hospital. They were shocked when they saw how much weight he had lost and how old he looked.[4] He gradually improved in the hospital, but his stay there lasted for months.

In response to questions about Mandela's health, the government of South Africa publicly announced that it did not intend to send him back to Pollsmoor Prison. Press releases did not, however, say if he would be freed. There were many rumors.

In December, the government announced that Mandela would remain a prisoner, but be transferred to a house at Victor Verster prison near Cape Town. The government wanted his family to live there with him. Mandela, however, would not allow his family to join him. He still wanted to be viewed as a prisoner, not as a leader who was getting special treatment. Although the move meant his living conditions vastly improved, he was very lonely in his new house. At least at Pollsmoor he had been able to mingle with other prisoners. Now the only people he had to talk to were guards. All his correspondence continued to be censored.

A New President

In September 1989, Frederik Willem de Klerk became the president of South Africa. In his inauguration speech, he talked of his hopes for a nonviolent transition to a nonracial South Africa. It was a big step. At the same time, de Klerk lifted the ban on the ANC. He also opened the way for the drafting of a new South African constitution.

In the months that followed, President de Klerk acted on his words. Neil Barnard was the government's intelligence chief at the time. Barnard arranged for talks between Mandela and the government. Mandela was finally offered terms he could accept. The government agreed his political activities could not be curtailed.

In December 1989, de Klerk made arrangements to see Mandela personally. They discussed his release.

On February 2, 1990, de Klerk delivered an address when the South African Parliament opened its annual session. He proposed a series of sweeping reforms. Eventually, he would lift the ban on all anti-apartheid groups, including the ANC and the Communist party. They would be allowed to operate as they chose. He also promised to open negotiations with the ANC, aimed at ending white control of the government. He would no longer permit prisoners to be executed. He would order the release of all political prisoners and grant exiles permission to return home. He wanted to restore blacks' civil rights. He would declare the state of emergency at an end. Immediate actions he took included desegregation of places like beaches and parks.

Freedom for Mandela and His People

President de Klerk announces the release of Nelson Mandela from prison on February 10, 1990.

Freedom!

On February 11, 1990, Nelson Mandela was released from prison. He had been locked up for twenty-seven years. Journalists and television reporters came from around the world to cover his release. Tens of millions of television viewers watched live as he walked through the prison gates, holding Winnie's hand.

By the time he was released, historian David Ottaway wrote:

> Mandela had been turned into a living legend, the symbol of the suffering of an entire black nation that had been uprooted from its homes, extorted of 87 percent of its land, and reduced to slave labor under the odious system of racial exploitation known as apartheid.[5]

His release created a great feeling of hope all over the world that conflict would soon give way to racial equality in South Africa.

Following his release, Mandela plunged back into South African politics. In 1991 members of the ANC elected him the organization's president. His personal life, however, was bringing him sadness. After thirty-four years of marriage, Nelson and Winnie Mandela divorced in 1992. His long imprisonment had been hard on his family, and the couple mutually decided to separate.

President Mandela

Apartheid finally ended in 1994. It had taken three years, from 1991 to 1994, for Afrikaners and blacks to draft a new constitution for the country of South Africa, one that guaranteed all citizens equal rights, regardless of race.

The world celebrated upon news of Mandela's release on February 11, 1990.

In 1994 the de Klerk government scheduled South Africa's first truly democratic elections, since adults of all races were allowed to take part. Over the course of three days, millions of South Africans went to the polls to cast their votes, which would decide who would serve in the nation's Parliament. It was a time of mixed emotions. At the end of the election, it was announced that Mandela's party, the African National Congress, had received 62 percent of the votes, and 252 seats in the National Assembly, compared with the National Party's 20 percent and 82 seats.[6] In South Africa, presidents are elected in the National Assembly. Mandela won the office, right after having voted in an election for the first time in his entire life.

During Mandela's term, the government worked to overcome the legacy of apartheid. Laws telling people what jobs they could hold or where they could live based on the color of their skin were eliminated. There were some advancements made in how people lived. During Mandela's presidency, 500,000 new homes would be built. Millions of old homes were equipped with electricity, water, and telephone lines.[7]

Despite significant progress, it would prove very difficult to reintegrate South African society. Observers in 1997 noted that most South African blacks continued to live in desperate poverty and in terrible conditions. Schools attended by black children still lacked basic necessities such as books and chalk. Some even had no windows.

However, for the first time in decades, the South African government was working to correct these problems of racial inequality. It would take an enormous amount of work and money, but many South Africans finally felt great hope that in time full equality would be achieved.

Primary Source: Preamble to the Constitution

We, the people of South Africa,

Recognise the injustices of our past;

Honour those who suffered for justice and freedom in our land;

Respect those who have worked to build and develop our country; and

Believe that South Africa belongs to all who live in it, united in our diversity.

We therefore, through our freely elected representatives, adopt this Constitution as the supreme law of the Republic so as to

- Heal the divisions of the past and establish a society based on democratic values, social justice and fundamental human rights;
- Lay the foundations for a democratic and open society in which government is based on the will of the people and every citizen is equally protected by law;
- Improve the quality of life of all citizens and free the potential of each person; and
- Build a united and democratic South Africa able to take its rightful place as a sovereign state in the family of nations.

May God protect our people.

Nkosi Sikelel' iAfrika. Morena boloka setjhaba sa heso.

God seën Suid-Afrika. God bless South Africa.

Mudzimu fhatutshedza Afurika. Hosi katekisa Afrika.

> *—The preamble of the current Constitution of South Africa, which was approved on December 4, 1996, established the rights of all South Africans.* [8]

In 1995 Mandela went to the World Cup rugby game and had the joy of awarding the cup to the winner, the South African team. He saw that as a moment when black-and-white South Africa could unite.

CHAPTER 9

In Retirement

According to the Constitution of South Africa, Nelson Mandela could have served two terms as president. But he was already an elderly man—seventy-five—when he was first elected to the office in 1994. Mandela did not want to accept a second term as president. During his presidency, he had had a very able deputy president, a fellow member of the ANC, Thabo Mbeki, who had handled many administrative responsibilities. In June of 1999, the people of South Africa went to the polls to elect a new Parliament. The ANC once again won a majority of seats in the Parliament. In South Africa, it is the National Assembly, the lower House in Parliament, which elects the nation's president. Mbeki ran unopposed for the office. Mandela beamed with happiness at Mbeki's election and his inauguration, on June 16.[1]

A very public figure for his entire adulthood, Mandela declared on stepping down from the presidency that he was looking forward to a quiet life. He wanted to have time to spend with his family—his children, his grandchildren, and his new wife, Graca Machel, a human rights activist in her own right.

NELSON MANDELA and the END of APARTHEID

Mandela spends time at his home in Qunu, where he retired after his term as president. Despite his official retirement, he remained active in South African causes like education and human rights.

In Retirement

Primary Source: Speech by Mandela

One of the things that made me long to be back in prison was that I had so little opportunity for reading, thinking and quiet reflection after my release. I intend, amongst other things, to give myself much more opportunity for such reading and reflection. And of course, there are those memoirs about the presidential years that now really need my urgent attention.

When I told one of my advisors a few months ago that I wanted to retire he growled at me: "you are retired." If that is really the case then I should say I now announce that I am retiring from retirement.

I do not intend to hide away totally from the public, but hence forth I want to be in the position of calling you to ask whether I would be welcome, rather than being called upon to do things and participate in events. The appeal therefore is: don't call me, I'll call you.[2]

–Mandela retires from public life in a speech given in June 2004.

The couple retired to Qunu, the town where he'd once lived with his mother. Mandela built two houses there, first a replica of the house he had lived in, in his final years in prison, and then a large mansion. He very much enjoyed the time he spent in the peaceful, quiet countryside. He spent time with people he had known since childhood, who remember how relaxed he looked, wearing a casual shirt and slacks rather than a prison uniform or suit. He found ways to help the people of the area, paying for renovations at a clinic and schools, for example.

Mandela remained very much in the public eye outside of Qunu as well. He was involved with the Nelson Mandela Foundation, founded in 1999. Dedicated to promoting peace, human rights, and democracy, it continues the great man's work to this day. Mandela made headlines again on February 11, 2000, when he celebrated the tenth anniversary of his release from prison. First he returned to the tiny village of Mvezo, in the Transkei region, where he was born. There, a monument was dedicated to mark the site of his birth. After the dedication ceremony, he and an entourage opened a new community museum and cultural center in Qunu. A museum dedicated to Mandela's life opened at the same time in Umtata.[3]

In 2000, he also appeared in the news when he lent his voice to a new cause, joining the fight against HIV/AIDS. By that point, South Africa had the highest rate of AIDS in the world.[5] That summer he was invited to give a speech at the XIII International AIDS Conference, which was held in South Africa. Between 2003 and 2008, world-famous musicians staged a series of concerts, named the 46664 concerts, in honor of Mandela (46664 was his prison number at Pollsmoor). In 2005, the world understood a little more

In Retirement

Primary Source: Recollections of Mandela's Personal Assistant

He always made his own bed, no matter where we traveled. I remember we were in Shanghai, in a very fancy hotel, and the Chinese hospitality requires that the person who cleans your room and provides you with your food, does exactly that. If you do it for yourself, it could even be regarded as an insult.

So in Shanghai I tried to say to him, "Please don't make your own bed, because there's this custom here." And he said, "Call them, bring them to me."

So I did. I asked the hotel manager to bring the ladies who would be cleaning the room, so that he could explain why he himself has to make his own bed, and that they not feel insulted. He didn't ever want to hurt people's feelings. He never really cared about what great big people think of him, but he did care about what small people thought of him.

–Deputy Secretary-General Jessie Duarte, Mandela's personal assistant from 1990 to 1994, recalls his kindness and humility.[4]

NELSON MANDELA and the END of APARTHEID

about why this issue was so important to Mandela, when it was announced that his only living son had died of AIDS-related complications.

During his early retirement years, Mandela remained involved in global affairs. In 1999 he was involved in negotiations with the Libyan government. These talks ended with two Libyan suspects in a terrorist bombing being deported to stand trial. Mandela also made efforts to bring about peace in Burundi, a war-torn country in east Africa. In 2007 he joined Richard Branson and Peter Gabriel in founding a group, called the Elders, which consists of global leaders who work together to promote peace and human rights. In 2009 Mandela's birthday was declared an international holiday by the United Nations.

By 2010, the world knew that Mandela's health was failing, but he still remained in the public eye. That year *Conversations with Myself* was published under his name. Sometimes described as Mandela's second autobiography, the book is really a collection or scrapbook of his earlier writings. Put together by a committee, it includes bits and pieces from journals, notebooks, letters, and speeches. Profits from the book went to the Nelson Mandela Foundation.[6]

In 2011 American First Lady Michelle Obama, along with her mother and two daughters, visited Mandela in South Africa. He had just published a book of his favorite folktales. In 2012 a movie based on Mandela's autobiography was released, also titled *A Long Walk to Freedom*. Just one week after the movie came out in South Africa, on December 5, 2013, South African President Jacob Zuma appeared on television late in the evening with news that would make headlines all over the world: Nelson Mandela, long-time political prisoner and the first president of a democratic

In Retirement

Mandela's death in 2013 brought about an outpouring of tributes and memorials to the great leader. Just one day after his burial, this statue of Mandela was unveiled in Pretoria, South Africa.

South Africa, had died at his home after a long battle with illness.

The world grieved. South Africa declared ten days of mourning. Heads of state from eighty different countries came to South Africa for the memorial service that was held on December 8. Nelson Mandela's body lay in state for three days, and was buried on December 15 in Qunu.

Today Mandela's is still a name known around the world. It seems likely he will be remembered for years to come, as one of the great liberators of all time.

TIMELINE

1918—Nelson Rolihlahla Mandela is born in the village of Mvezo, Umtata, in the Transkei territory.

1927—Mandela's father, Gadla Henry Mphakanyiswa, dies; Nelson goes to live with the tribe's king, Jongintaba.

1940—Mandela is expelled from University College at Fort Hare for taking part in a student strike; escaping marriages arranged by his foster father, he and his foster brother flee to Johannesburg; Mandela finds work in a law firm.

1944—Mandela joins the African National Congress (ANC); helps form the radical Youth League within the ANC; marries Evelyn Mase.

1948—The National Party takes power with the avowed purpose of instituting the system of racial discrimination called apartheid.

1950—The ANC joins forces with other anti-apartheid groups, including the Communist party.

1952—Mandela establishes his law practice; orchestrates a defiance campaign for the ANC, a nonviolent demonstration against apartheid; is arrested for the first time and receives a suspended sentence.

1953—The government bans Nelson Mandela from participating in the ANC.

1956—Mandela is arrested for a second time, charged with treason; he is released until sentencing.

1957—Mandela divorces Evelyn Mase.

1958—Mandela marries Winnie Madikizela.

1960—Black protesters are gunned down by white policemen when they gather in Sharpeville;

Mandela and other members of the ANC are arrested in the wake of protests following Sharpeville; they are charged with treason.

NELSON MANDELA and the END of APARTHEID

1961—**March:** Mandela and his codefendants are found not guilty in the Treason Trial; Mandela goes underground.

December 16: The radical political group, Umkhonto we Sizwe, bombs power plants and government buildings.

1962—Mandela is captured by the police and thrown in prison to await trial.

1964—Mandela is sentenced to life in prison on charges of sabotage and conspiracy to overthrow the government by violence.

1970s—Violence erupts in South Africa as black activists fight whites and other blacks they suspect of cooperating with Afrikaners.

1973—South African government offers Mandela release in exchange for a promise that he will not participate in the anti-apartheid movement; he refuses the offer.

1978—Pieter Botha becomes the new South African president; he talks of the possibility of abolishing apartheid but fails to take any significant steps toward doing so.

1980s—South Africa receives constant pressure from other nations to release Mandela.

1981—United States congressmen petition for an interview with Mandela, but their request is denied; Mandela has become a symbol of the fight for human rights.

1982—Mandela is transferred to Pollsmoor Prison, near Cape Town.

1989—Mandela meets with South Africa's new president, Frederik Willem de Klerk.

1990—Nelson Mandela is released from prison after twenty-seven years.

1992—Nelson and Winnie Mandela divorce.

Timeline

1993—Nelson Mandela and de Klerk receive the Nobel Peace Prize for their efforts to end apartheid in South Africa.

1994—Nelson Mandela is elected president of South Africa; the election signals the end of apartheid.

1998—Nelson Mandela remarries, to Graca Machel.

1999—Nelson Mandela decides not to run for a second term as president. South African voters elect Thabo Mbeki, another ANC leader, president in a landslide.

2012—The world learns that Mandela is not in good health.

2013—Mandela dies and the world mourns.

CHAPTER NOTES

CHAPTER 1. An End to a Fight—and a Peace Prize

1. Francis Sejersted, "Nobel Peace Prize 1993—Presentation Speech," *Nobelprize.org*, 1993, http://www.nobelprize.org/nobel_prizes/peace/laureates/1993/presentation-speech.html (accessed June 29, 2015).
2. Ibid.
3. Nelson Mandela, *Long Walk to Freedom* (Boston: Little, Brown and Company, 1994), p. 544.
4. Ibid.

CHAPTER 2. South Africa's Past

1. Central Intelligence Agency, "Country Comparison: Population," *World Factbook*, https://www.cia.gov/library/publications/the-world-factbook/rankorder/2119rank.html (accessed June 29, 2015).
2. "Poverty Levels Dropping in South Africa: Report," *SouthAfrica.info,* April 4, 2014. http://www.southafrica.info/about/social/poverty-040414.htm#.VZHydflViko.
3. "The Dutch Settlement," *South African History Online,"* http://www.sahistory.org.za/cape-town/dutch-settlement (accessed June 29, 2015).
4. Robert Ross, "Khoesan and Immigrants: The Emergence of Colonial Society in the Cape, 1500–1800," in Carolyn Hamilton, Bernard Mbenga, and Robert Ross, eds., *Cambridge History of South Africa* (Cambridge, England: Cambridge University Press, 2010), vol. 1, p. 175.
5. "The First Slaves at the Cape," *South African History Online,* http://www.sahistory.org.za/article/first-slaves-cape (accessed June 29, 2015).
6. John Wright, "Turbulent Times: Political Transformation in the North and East, 1760s–1830s," in Hamilton, vol. 1, p. 217.
7. Padraig O'Malley, "Ordinance 50," *Nelson Mandela Centre of Memory,* https://www.nelsonmandela.org/omalley/index.

Chapter Notes

   php/site/q/03lv01538/04lv01646/05lv01658.htm (accessed June 29, 2015).
8. "The Story of Africa: Southern Africa," *BBC World Service*, http://www.bbc.co.uk/worldservice/africa/features/storyofafrica/12chapter2.shtml (accessed June 29, 2015).
9. Norman Etherington, Patrick Harries, and Bernard K. Mbenga, "From Colonial Hegemonies to Imperial Conquest, 1840–1880," Hamilton, vol. 1, p. 324.
10. "The War," *South Africa History Online*, http://www.sahistory.org.za/war (accessed June 29, 2015).
11. "Black Concentration Camps During Anglo-Boer War," *South Africa History Online*, http://www.sahistory.org.za/topic/black-concentration-camps-during-anglo-boer-war-2-1900-1902 (accessed June 29, 2015).

CHAPTER 3. A Young Nelson Mandela

1. "Qunu: The Place Where Nelson Mandela Was at Home," *The Guardian*, December 6, 2013, http://www.theguardian.com/world/2013/dec/06/qunu-nelson-mandela-home.
2. Monica Hunter, *Reaction to Conquest: Effects of Contact with Europeans on the Pondo of South Africa* (Cape Town: David Philip, 1979), p. 25.
3. C.H. Feinstein, *An Economic History of South Africa* (London: Cambridge University Press, 2005), p. 152.
4. Nelson Mandela, *Long Walk to Freedom* (Boston: Little, Brown and Company, 1994), p. 6.
5. Ibid., p. 10.
6. Hunter, p. 175.
7. Mandela, pp. 12–13.
8. Ibid., p. 13.
9. Ibid., p. 14.
10. Ibid., p. 41.

CHAPTER 4. The Rise of Apartheid

1. William Bernart, *Twentieth-Century South Africa*, 2nd ed. (Oxford, England: Oxford University Press, 2001), p. 146.
2. "The 1936 Census of the Union of South Africa," *JSTOR*, http://www.jstor.org/stable/2730411 (accessed June 30, 2015).
3. Leonard Thompson, *History of South Africa*, 4th ed. (New Haven, CT: Yale University Press, 2014), p. 175.
4. "Industrial and Commercial Workers Union," *South Africa History Online*, http://www.sahistory.org.za/organisations/industrial-and-commercial-workers-union-icu (accessed June 30, 2015).
5. Nelson Mandela, *Long Walk to Freedom* (Boston: Back Bay Books, 2013), p. 90.
6. "Rejuvenation of the ANC and Intensification of the Struggle, 1940s," *South Africa History Online*, http://www.sahistory.org.za/topic/rejuvenation-anc-and-intensification-struggle-1940s (accessed June 30, 2015).
7. John Carlin, "Interview: Walter Sisulu," http://www.pbs.org/wgbh/pages/frontline/shows/mandela/interviews/sisulu.html (accessed June 30, 2015).
8. Mandela, p. 104.

CHAPTER 5. Apartheid—"Apartness"

1. Tim McKee and Anne Blackshaw, *No More Strangers Now: Young Voices from a New South Africa* (New York: DK Publishing, Inc., 1998), p. xv.
2. Hannah Britton, *Women in the South African Parliament* (Urbana: University of Illinois Press, 2005), p. 9.
3. "Statement by the National Party of South Africa, May 29, 1948," *Modern History Sourcecook*, http://legacy.fordham.edu/halsall/mod/1948apartheid1.html (accessed June 25, 2015).

Chapter Notes

4. Michael Morris and John Linnegar, *Every Step of the Way* (Cape Town, South Africa: HSRC Press, 2004), p. 162.
5. Nelson Mandela, *Long Walk to Freedom* (Boston: Little, Brown and Company, 1994), p. 97.
6. Ibid., 102.

CHAPTER 6. Fighting Back

1. ANC Adopts Programme of Action," *South Africa History Online*, http://www.sahistory.org.za/dated-event/anc-adopts-programme-action (accessed June 30, 2015).
2. David James Smith, *Young Mandela: The Revolutionary Years* (New York: Little, Brown, 2010), first page of chapter 6, e-book.
3. Michael Morris and John Linnegar, *Every Step of the Way* (Cape Town, South Africa: HSRC Press, 2004), p. 162.
4. "Defiance Campaign 1952," *South Africa History Online*, http://www.sahistory.org.za/topic/defiance-campaign-1952 (accessed June 30, 2015).
5. Padraig O'Malley, "The Freedom Charter, 26 June 1955," *Nelson Mandela Centre of Memory*, https://www.nelsonmandela.org/omalley/index.php/site/q/03lv01538/04lv01600/05lv01611/06lv01612.htm (accessed June 29, 2015).
6. Frannie Rabkin, "Mandela Respected the Law in Fight for Freedom," *Business Daily Live*, December 11, 2013, http://www.bdlive.co.za/national/law/2013/12/11/mandela-respected-the-law-in-fight-for-freedom (accessed June 30, 2015).
7. Nelson Mandela, *Long Walk to Freedom* (Boston: Back Bay Books, 2013), p. 259.
8. Humphrey Tyler, "Africans' Gaiety Ended by Bullets," *New York Times*, April 3, 1960, http://query.nytimes.com/mem/archive/pdf?res=9907EED91E3DEF3ABC4B53DFB266838B679EDE.f

CHAPTER 7. **Arrested and Imprisoned**

1. Nelson Mandela, *Long Walk to Freedom* (Boston: Little, Back Bay Books, 2013), p. 274.
2. "A Brief History of the African National Congress," *African National Congress,* http://www.anc.org.za/show.php?id=206 (accessed June 30, 2015).
3. Washington State University Department of English, "Umkhonto we Sizwe (Military Wing of the African National Congress): We Are at War! (December 16, 1961)," *Reading About the World,* December 23, 1998, http://public.wsu.edu/~brians/world_civ/worldcivreader/world_civ_reader_2/umkhonto.html.
4. Nelson Mandela, "An Ideal for Which I Am Prepared to Die," *The Guardian,* April 23, 2007, http://www.theguardian.com/world/2007/apr/23/nelsonmandela.
5. Steven Biko, "The Definition of Black Consciousness, [December 1971]" *South Africa History Online,* http://www.sahistory.org.za/archive/definition-black-consciousness-bantu-stephen-biko-december-1971-south-africa (accessed June 30, 2015).
6. John Dugard, "Convention on the Suppression and Punishment of the Crime of Apartheid," *United Nations Audiovisual Library of International Law,* http://legal.un.org/avl/ha/cspca/cspca.html (accessed June 30, 2015).
7. "Nelson Mandela," *South African History Online,* http://v1.sahistory.org.za/pages/people/special%20projects/mandela/timeline_8.htm (accessed August 19, 2015).

CHAPTER 8. **Freedom for Mandela and His People**

1. Michigan State University African Studies Department, et al., "Soweto Student Uprising," *South Africa: Overcoming Apartheid, Building Democracy,* http://overcomingapartheid.msu.edu/sidebar.php?id=65-258-3 (accessed June 30, 2015).

Chapter Notes

2. L.M. Thompson, *A History of South Africa* (New Haven, CT: Yale University, 1990), p. 215.
3. Nelson Mandela, *Long Walk to Freedom* (Boston: Little, Brown and Company, 1994), p. 464.
4. "Mandela's Condition Improving," *Chicago Tribune*, August 15, 1988, http://articles.chicagotribune.com/1988-08-15/news/8801220867_1_winnie-mandela-ismail-ayob-tygerberg-hospital.
5. David Ottaway, *Chained Together: Mandela, de Klerk, and the Struggle to Remake South Africa* (New York: Times Books, 1993), p. 11.
6. "South Africa Election Results 1994," *Election Resources on the Internet: Republic of South Africa General Election Results Lookup,* http://electionresources.org/za/provinces.php?election=1994 (accessed June 30, 2015).
7. Suzanne Daley, "At Inauguration, Mbeki Calls for Rebirth of South Africa," *New York Times*, June 17, 1999, http://www.nytimes.com/1999/06/17/world/at-inauguration-mbeki-calls-for-rebirth-of-south-africa.html.
8. "Constitution of the Republic of South Africa, 1996—Preamble," http://www.gov.za/documents/constitution-republic-south-africa-1996-preamble (accessed August 11, 2015).

CHAPTER 9. In Retirement

1. Suzanne Daley, "Mandela, With Touch of Grace, Paves Way for Successor," *New York Times*, June 15, 1999, http://www.nytimes.com/1999/06/15/world/mandela-with-touch-of-grace-paves-way-for-successor.html.
2. "Nelson Mandela's Five Most Memorable Speeches,"*Firstpost*, December 6, 2013, http://www.firstpost.com/world/nelson-mandelas-five-most-memorable-speeches-1270759.html.

3. "Qunu, the Beloved Rural Childhood Home of Mandela," *Times Live,* December 12, 2013, http://www.timeslive.co.za/local/2013/12/06/qunu-the-beloved-rural-childhood-home-of-mandela.
4. Kharunya Paramaguru, "5 Great Stories about Nelson Mandela's Humility, Kindness and Courage," *Time,* December 6, 2013, http://world.time.com/2013/12/06/5-great-stories-about-nelson-mandelas-humility-kindness-and-courage/.
5. "How Nelson Mandela Changed the AIDS Agenda in South Africa, *The Guardian,* December 6, 2013, http://www.theguardian.com/world/2013/dec/06/nelson-mandela-aids-south-africa.
6. "Nelson Mandela Anguished over Family's Suffering, Says Book," *The Guardian,* October 11, 2010, http://www.theguardian.com/world/2010/oct/11/nelson-mandela-conversations-with-myself.

GLOSSARY

activist—An especially vocal and vigorous advocate of a cause, especially a political cause.

Afrikaans—An official language in South Africa, that is very much like Dutch.

Afrikaner—A person born in South Africa, of European (generally Dutch) descent, who speaks the Afrikaans language.

apartheid—From the Afrikaans language, apartness. The South African policy or system of segregation by race.

colony—A place that is occupied and ruled by people from another country, typically far away.

Coloured—Used in South Africa to mean a person of mixed race. *Colored* is an offensive term in the United States, but *coloured* is still used by the South African government, when collecting data for the census, for example.

concentration camp—A camp where persons (prisoners of war, political prisoners, or refugees) are forced to live.

constraints—Limitations or restrictions.

defiance—Open resistance.

discrimination—Unfair treatment, based on a person's race, age, or sex, for example.

guerrillas—Members of a small independent group taking part in irregular fighting, typically against larger regular forces (like the police or an army).

missionaries—Religious people who go, usually to a foreign land, to try to convert natives to Christianity.

pass—A permit to enter a place.

protest—An objection to something a person has little control over.

radical—Complete; extreme.

reserve—A place set apart, sometimes where one particular type of people are forced to live.

resistance—The refusal to accept something.

segregation—Separation by race. Practiced in the United States and elsewhere in the past.

self-rule—Self-government, mostly used when a nation has once been a colony.

trek—An extremely long journey.

underground—In hiding. Used when an individual or group fights a government or policy from secret locations.

FURTHER READING

Books
Dakers, Diane. *Nelson Mandela: South Africa's Anti-Apartheid Revolutionary.* New York: Crabtree, 2014.

Keller, Bill. Tree Shaker: *The Story of Nelson Mandela.* Boston: Kingfisher, 2013.

Mandela, Nelson. *Long Walk to Freedom.* Boston: Little, Brown and Company, 1994.

Nelson, Kadir. *Nelson Mandela.* New York: Katherine Tegen Books, 2013.

Noonan, Sheila Smith. *South Africa.* Broomall, PA: Mason Crest, 2012.

Senker, Cath. *Mandela and Truth and Reconciliation.* Chicago: Heinemann, 2013.

Websites

Overcoming Apartheid
overcomingapartheid.msu.edu/index.php
Features many personal narratives and historical essays.

Mandela: An Audio History
www.mandelahistory.org
A five-part audio history broadcast that includes recordings of Mandela and others involved in the fight against apartheid.

Nelson Mandela Foundation
www.nelsonmandela.org
Includes biography, timeline, advocacy, and opportunities to get involved.

Life and Legacy of Nelson Mandela
www.nytimes.com/interactive/2013/12/05/world/africa/Mandela-Timeline.html
Provides a timeline of Mandela's life, with links to articles about featured events.

Apartheid Timeline
www.pbs.org/wgbh/masterpiece/endgame/timeline.html
Highlights important events in the history of apartheid.

INDEX

A

African National Congress, 51, 54–55, 57, 63–64, 66, 67–68, 70–71, 73, 75, 77, 81, 83–84, 88, 95, 98, 100, 102, 105
    Programme of Action, 67
    Youth League, 55, 57, 63–64, 66
African Resistance Movement, 81, 87
Afrikaans, 8, 17, 22–24, 26, 48, 60, 68, 93
Afrikaners
    attitude toward British rule, 19, 21, 22–24, 26, 47
    colonize South Africa, 14–15, 17–19, 21
    establish independent republics, 22–24, 26, 28, 89
    fight British in South African War, 26–29
    political role, 47–48, 51
apartheid
    ends, 29, 93, 95, 97–98, 100, 102–103
    established, 58–60, 62–63
    protests, 9–10, 33, 51–52, 55, 63–64, 66, 68, 70–71, 75, 77, 79, 81, 90, 92–93, 95
    world reaction, 8–9, 75, 87–90, 92, 93, 95

B

Barnard, Neil, 98
Biko, Steve, 89, 95
black consciousness, 89
Black Sash, 63
Boer War. *See* South African War
Botha, Louis, 47
Botha, Pieter Willem, 9, 93, 95, 97
Branson, Richard, 110

C

Campaign for the Defiance of Unjust Laws, 68, 70
Cape Colony, 19, 21, 23–24, 26, 29
Churchill, Winston, 55
Coloured (minority), 11, 18, 28, 51, 58–59, 68, 73, 93, 95
Communism/Communist Party, 52, 54, 63–64, 77, 90, 98
Congress of Democrats, 73
Congress of the People, 71

D

da Gama, Vasco, 14
Dalindyebo, Jongintaba, 38, 40–41, 43, 52, 54
Defiance Campaign, 67, 70–74
de Klerk, Frederik W., 7–10, 98, 102
Diaz, Bartholomew, 14
Dutch. *See* Afrikaners
Dutch East India Company, 15, 17, 19, 22

E

European exploration of South Africa, 13–15, 17–19, 21–24, 26–29

G

Gabriel, Peter, 10
Great Britain
    fights South African War, 26–29
    seizes control of Cape Colony, 19, 21, 23–24, 26, 29
    settlers arrive, 19, 21, 23–24, 27
    severs relations with South Africa, 89
Great Depression, 48
Great Trek, 22–24, 26

H

Haarlem, 15
Hertzog, J.B.M., 47J

126

Index

Hitler, Adolf, 48
Houtman, Cornelius, 14

I
Indian (minority), 23, 23, 28, 51, 59, 67–68, 71, 93, 95
Industrial and Commercial Worker Union (ICU), 52

J
Jongintaba, 38, 40–41, 43, 52, 54

K
Karrir War, 19
Khoikhoi (or Hottentots), 13–15, 17–19
Kruger, Paul, 26

L
Luthuli, Albert, 75, 83

M
Machel, Graca, 105
Macmillan, Harold, 89
Madikizela, Winnie Nomzano, 73, 83, 85, 87, 97, 100
Malan, Danielle, 68
Mandela, Nelson
  African National Congress, 54–55, 57, 63–64, 66, 67–68, 70–71, 73, 75, 77, 81, 83, 88, 95, 98, 100, 105
  appearance, 7
  arrested, 8, 70–71, 73, 77, 81, 83, 85
  childhood, 30, 32–34, 36–38, 40–41
  death, 110, 112
  education, 37, 40–41, 43–44, 52, 54–55, 60, 62
  elected president of South Africa, 100, 102
  family, 34, 36–38, 40–41, 52, 62–64, 73, 97, 100, 105
  imprisoned, 70–71, 77, 81, 83–85, 87–90, 92, 97, 98
  lawyer, 62–64, 71
  life underground, 80–81, 83
  marriage to Evelyn Mase, 62–63, 73
  marriage to Graca Machel, 105
  marriage to Winnie Nomzano Madikizela, 73, 83, 85, 97, 97, 100
  name, 30, 32, 36–37
  receives Nobel Peace Prize, 7–10
  release from prison, 9, 97–98, 100, 107–108
  retirement, 105, 108, 110, 112
  symbolic figure, 8–9, 90, 92, 100
  trials, 70–71, 73, 77, 80, 87–88
  writings, 110
Mandela, Nonqaphi Nosekeni Fanny (mother), 32, 34, 36–38, 87, 108
Mase, Evelyn, 62–63, 73
Mbeki, Thabo, 105
Milner, Alfred, 27
Mines and Works Act of 1911, 33
Moroka, James, 67–68
Mphakanyiswa, Gadla Henry (father), 32–34, 36–38

N
National Union of South African Students' Organization, 89
Nationalists (National Party), 47–48, 58–60, 63, 68, 73, 79, 89, 102
native South Africans
  ancient times, 11, 13
  apartheid, 29, 44–45, 47–48, 50–52, 58–60, 62–64, 66
  attitudes toward European colonists, 22–24, 26
  conditions after apartheid, 13, 100, 102
  conflict with Dutch settlers, 15, 17–18

granted civil rights by British, 21
resistance, 18, 67–68, 81, 87, 90, 95
right to vote, 9, 27–29, 47, 50, 58, 102
segregation, 7, 28–29, 33, 41, 45, 50–51, 58, 68, 98
Natives Land Act of 1913, 33, 50
Nelson Mandela Foundation, 108, 110
Nobel Peace Prize, 7, 8, 10, 88
Nokwe, Duma, 75

O
Obama, Michelle, 110
Orange Free State, 23, 26, 28
Organization of African Unity, 83

P
PanAfricans, 54
Pan-Africanist Congress (PAC), 73, 75, 77, 81, 85, 87, 95
pass laws, 50, 58, 75
Peace of Vereeniging, 26
Portugal, 13–14

R
Radebe, Gaur, 54–55
Rhodes, Cecil, 24, 26
Roosevelt, Franklin D., 55

S
Seme, Pixley, 66
Sharpeville Massacre, 75, 79
Sisulu, Walter, 54–55, 57, 62, 67–68
slavery, 17–19, 22, 58, 84, 100
Smuts, Jan Christiaan, 43–44, 47–48
Sobukwe, Robert Mangaliso, 73
South Africa
 ancient history, 11, 13
 exploration, 13–15, 17–18
 geography, 11, 13
 politics, 43, 55, 64, 100
 population, 11, 13, 17–18, 22–23
 unification, 27–28, 33

South African Coloured People's Organization, 73
South African Congress of Trade Unions, 73
South African Indian Congress, 51, 67, 71, 73
South African Native Trust, 50
South African Parliament, 89, 93, 102, 105
South African Students' Organization, 89, 95
South African War, 26–29
Soweto, 93, 95
Suppression of Communism Act, 64

T
Tambo, Oliver, 67, 71, 77
Transvaal War, 24, 26
Treason Trial, 77, 80

U
Umkhonto we Sizwe, 81, 83–84, 87
Union of South Africa. *See* South Africa
United Nations (UN), 75, 89 110
United Party, 48
Urban Areas Acts of 1923, 33

V
van Riebeeck, Jan, 15

W
Williams, Cecil, 83
World War I, 30, 32, 47, 51
World War II, 43–44, 48

X
Xhosa, 18–19, 21, 23, 30, 36, 40
Xuma, Alfred B., 55, 66–67

Z
Zulu, 22, 26
Zuma, Jacob, 110